Value Investing:
A Disciplined Framework

By

Tyler Hardt, CFA

Value Investing: A Disciplined Framework

ISBN: 9798654494726
Imprint: Independently published

Cover Design by: Tyler Hardt

Printed in the United States of America

This book is dedicated to my wife and loving family

Contents

Page 4   **Introduction**
Page 11   **Principals of Value Investing**
Page 32   **Discipline Fundamentals and Human**
                Behavior
Page 41   **Value Investing Framework**
Page 60   **Additional Investing Topics**
Page 70   **Conclusion**
Page 73   **Value Investing Framework in Action**
Page 74   **Rockwell Automation (ROK)**
Page 83   **Diamond Offshore (DO)**
Page 94   **Carpenter Technologies**

Introduction

In the early 1980's after enduring oil embargos, markets that went nowhere, and crushing inflation; a hopeful America shed its negative impressions of stocks, giving way to the rise of a new investor class. Only a few years after Business Week magazine infamously proclaimed the "death of equities", the popularity of investing grew to a near frenzy as a culture of star-portfolio managers and dot-com billionaires pervaded society. Talk around the water cooler shifted from Monday Night Football to the latest hot stock tips. IPO, ETF, and IRA joined the American lexicon. Pictures of Microsoft's janitors standing in front of their Lamborghinis and Ferraris captured the imaginations of everyone.

Seemingly at once, the nation woke up to the realization that the best path to building wealth was investing in stocks.

Individual investors opened new brokerage accounts by the millions. The public was bombarded by constant television commercials from the likes of Charles Schwab and Fidelity. In a significant structural shift of market participation, a majority of families began taking control of their own financial future through IRA's and 401(k)'s. Employers enthusiastically complied and happily shifted the burden of funding retirements from their balance sheets to their employees.

The flood gates opened and individual retail investors were given access to information and self-brokerage services that democratized what was once perceived as an exclusive club. Participating in the markets became easier as the internet provided real time quotes, and brokerage houses slashed commissions from north of seventy five dollars a trade to a mere eight bucks. With a click of a mouse, anyone with a bank account could purchase options, futures, commodities, currencies, and stocks in over a dozen foreign markets. We all became market experts. Just like our assessment of our driving skills (I'm an above average driver thank you very much), each of us began to believe that we could beat the market averages. In the midst of this investor revolution, "Day Trader" became a legitimate job title.

Investors began scrutinizing market returns in continuously compressed time intervals. People began following their stocks monthly, daily, and hourly. No longer was a quarterly brokerage statement sent by mail deemed satisfactory. In the 1980's, a quick mention of the closing price of the Dow Jones Industrial Index on the nightly news was considered sufficient. In the opening decade of the twenty first century,

CNBC began broadcasting directly from the floor of the New York Stock Exchange; filming ultra-busy traders scurrying between celebrity hosts whose eyes constantly wander off camera to follow the latest market quotes. Mutual funds that are only priced once a day became inadequate and lost their luster to a new investment vehicle called exchange traded funds (ETF's), which were essentially mutual funds quoted continuously through out the trading day. These ETF's also allowed quick minded "active" investors to circumvent short term trading fees levied by mutual funds.

Americans were hooked on investing, and they craved options. Wall Street saw dollar signs and more than happily obliged with a plethora of products and investment vehicles, promoting hundreds of market beating strategies, which contradictorily all claimed to be superior to one another.

Today there are tens of thousands of mutual funds, ETF's and hedge funds. Some of which even boast that their fund's investment strategy is based on the recommendations of a "black box", and they may only hold a position for mere seconds (I may be old fashioned, but I still equate black boxes with aviation disasters, and I find the use of the "black box" label as a way to describe an investment strategy somewhat ironic and alarming). ETF's at first tracked major market indices, but their fast success lead to an explosion of ETF options that track slices and niches of every market sector conceivable. There are even ETF's that use two or three times leverage and short the market or individual sectors.

Of course, Wall Street congratulated themselves for this triumph of progress and innovation. These products were voraciously promoted and each proclaimed to beat the market. But in reality few did, as performance was eaten away by mounting trading costs and added layers of advisory fees.[1] The rapid development of alternative investment vehicles also lead to an increasing complexity, as money managers tried to invent a better mouse trap. Given these facts it's not surprising that index funds have exploded in popularity as investors' threw up their hands in response to complexity and high fees that made it near impossible to beat the market averages.

In what can best be blamed on human nature, the majority of investors simply get carried away by the constant drumbeat of excitement from Wall Street and the toxic allure of making a quick fortune. Our inability to focus on the long-term combined with the need for instant gratification led many astray from the primary reason they began investing in the first place; preservation of capital and increasing wealth in an effort to secure an adequate nest-egg for a comfortable retirement. The tried and true strategy of patient accumulation of undervalued quality companies was simply drowned out by Wall Street and the popular press.

The majority of investing and trading strategies come and go with the frequency of a new moon. They usually enrich the strategy's promoter and brokerage houses, but seldom independent investors. Conversely, the principles of value

---

[1] In his 2006 shareholder letter, Warren Buffett eloquently detailed how Wall Street has captured 20% of investor's wealth through layers of fees through his fable of the "Gotrocks".

investing have stood the test of time and avoided being labeled a fad.

The fundamentals of value investing, first described by Ben Graham and David Dodd in the throws of the Great Depression, have proven themselves to be successful over decades, through the ups and downs of numerous business cycles and bull and bear markets.[2] The key to the longevity and success of value investing is that it doesn't rely on complexity or cutting edge trading formulas, but rather the principles of common sense, patience, discipline, and independent thinking. The practitioners of value investing have beaten the market averages over decades with much less anxiety and risk than other investors. Famed value investor Christopher Browne once quipped to a group of Wharton Students that "stress kills people and because of this value investors simply live longer".[3]

In the pages that follow I will discuss the fundamental principles of value investing, and form a complete framework for identifying attractive stocks that should generate handsome returns. I must stress that this isn't some secret formula. In fact, successful value investors have talked openly about their investment strategies in newspapers, magazines, and books for decades. I will even share a compilation of investment strategies from some of the

---

[2] The first edition of *Security Analysis* was written by Benjamin Graham and David Dodd in 1934, and is considered by many practitioners as the "Bible of value investing".

[3] Christopher Browne, portfolio manager of Tweedy, Browne Co., lecturing at a Wharton Investment Management Club's Speaker Series in the spring 2008.

world's best value investors in their own words. The similarity in the descriptions of their investing strategies is a testament to the commonality of the core principles of value investing that I will focus on in this paper.

In essence, value investors buy the stocks of high quality companies that have sustainable earnings, little or no debt, pay dividends, and whose stock trades for undemanding multiples.[4] The framework to execute this approach is comprised of four steps;

1. Identify companies with moats
2. Evaluate financial strength
3. Estimate the value of shares
4. Wait for the margin of safety

But prior to detailing the specifics of this framework, I am going to reinforce the need for strong personal discipline when investing. Having a focused investor mentality will be crucial to your success and the ability to appropriately employ a value oriented investment strategy. This essential foundation includes: independent thinking, patience, and financial discipline. There are many human behavioral characteristics that have subconscious effects on the decision making process. Every investor should be cognizant of these biases and more importantly able to recognize when they are affecting their investment decision process.

---

[4] An "undemanding" multiple is a reference to a stock's price-to-earnings (P/E) multiple, which is less than the long-run average for the market's normalized P/E multiple (which is approx. 15x), while taking into account the company's earnings growth and leverage. I credit the phrase "undemanding multiple" to Jim Kieffer of Artisan Partners, L.P.

Value Investing: A Disciplined Framework

It is extremely important to understand that successful value investing is the marriage of the ability to identify and invest in undervalued companies **AND** that individual's ability to exercise self control with a sound disciplined behavior. Successful investing and prudent discipline are not mutually exclusive.

I will conclude with brief discussions of several additional investing topics and their application in the value investment framework. These topics will include: the importance of dividends, thoughts on diversification, tactics for avoiding value traps, and others.

Hopefully, you will find the contents of the remaining pages insightful and easily applicable for developing or refining your investment strategy. The majority of principles and insights should appear more common sense than financial wizardry. Common sense is the central tenant of value investing, and quite frankly common sense is severely absent on Wall Street. While it may not be as sexy as matching pairs trades, value investing is financially rewarding and a proven strategy to preserve capital and grow your wealth.[5]

---

[5] A pairs trade is a strategy typically utilized by hedge funds where they would invest in the stocks of two very similar competitors, such as Home Depot and Lowes, and buy the underperforming stock and sell the outperforming stock. The investor is essentially betting that the "spread" between the two will eventually converge. In a pairs trade, you are not making a bet on the direction of the stocks in absolute terms, but on the direction of the stocks relative to each other.

Principles of Value Investing

Ben Graham and David Dodd first introduced the concept of value investing in their seminal work, "Security Analysis", in which they articulated the fundamentals and techniques necessary for selecting profitable investments. Over the last seventy five years these principles have remained unchanged and proven to be tremendously successful in practice.

Many investors have adopted Graham and Dodd's framework as a foundation for their own investment strategies. Investors who have applied this value-oriented approach to stock selection have profited handsomely, and include: Warren Buffett, Seth Klarman, Christopher Browne, Marty Whitman, Bill Ruane, Charlie Munger, and Walter Schloss. Collectively, this group represents some of the world's greatest investors. Over long time periods these disciples of Graham and Dodd have managed to earn returns in excess of the market averages, something that most market observers and academics consider impossible because they believe that markets are efficient.[6]

The Efficient Market Hypothesis postulates that all available information is assessed by market participants and instantly incorporated into security prices.[7] Of course, this theory implies that all investors are rational and that the current market price of any security represents the one and only true market value. Consequently, it is impossible over long periods of time to beat the market averages, and anyone who does is simply lucky.

I believe there are three major flaws in the intuition behind this theory. Firstly, security prices are based on *estimates* of future cash flows and are therefore not based on available information, but rather each individual's *interpretation* of that information. Remember that "estimate" is a polite word for "guess" and is subject to opinion and error. Moreover,

---

[6] In 1984 Warren Buffett gave a speech titled "The Superinvestors of Graham-and-Doddsville" at Columbia University in which he countered arguments that markets are efficient, and the fact that he has managed to beat the market was only an aberration, likened to flipping a coin 20 times and always landing heads up (statistically possible but extremely unlikely). Buffett acknowledged that if he was the only person who had beaten the market than it would be luck. However, the fact that several investors all practicing the same investment strategy as described in "Security Analysis" by Graham and Dodd each beating the market could not be passed off as an aberration or luck, and that markets are not always efficient.
[7] The Efficient Market Hypothesis was first proposed in the 1960's by Professor Eugene Fama at the University of Chicago.

just because information is available doesn't mean everyone uses it. Secondly, the theory assumes that human behavior is rational and free from emotion. Unfortunately, when most investors make an investment decision their mental process is governed by fear and greed, strong emotions that will often override rational thinking. Lastly, the theory assumes that all investors are the same. However, investors have different risk appetites, intellectual capabilities, and levels of investing experience. Some people invest to save for retirement, others because it's their business. You can never know which marginal investors are driving stock prices. Bill Ruane describes the impact of this last flaw better than I ever could. He explains; "In this business you have investors, imitators, and the swarming incompetents. Occasionally the imitators and swarming incompetents take the market's wheel and either drive it to excess or cut prices in half."[8]

The most obvious flaw in the Efficient Market Hypothesis is the fact that it doesn't work in the real world.[9] Markets are simply not always efficient and every once in a while assets can become grossly mispriced. This is because people often use mental short cuts called heuristics to make complicated decisions based on prior experience without the full analysis required by the rational investor. One common heuristic that allows value investing to beat the market is called "representativeness", which is when investors assume past

---

[8] Schroeder, Alice (2008). *The Snowball: Warren Buffett and the Business of Life*. New York: Bantam Dell, page 405.
[9] For more info on empirical evidence that summarizes how the Efficient Market Hypothesis is unable to explain real market pricing behavior, please see "The Efficient Market Hypothesis: A Survey" by Meredith Beechey, et. al. (http://ideas.repec.org/p/rba/rbardp/rdp2000-01.html)

performance to be representative of future performance. This results in stocks becoming overvalued when times are good, and undervalued when times are bad creating investment opportunities for value investors. It is important to recognize that abnormally good or bad conditions don't last forever.[10]

However, eventually arbitragers will eliminate some biases that lead to asset mispricing. But they will not immediately eliminate every market mispricing because it can be difficult and costly to short stocks, or more often the arbitrageurs simply can't outweigh the momentum of the crowd and the mispricing can persist.

Research by Richard Thaler of the University of Chicago found that in the late 1990's hedge fund managers believed that internet stocks were grossly overvalued, but they would continue to hold them as they believed irrational exuberance would further push prices higher.[11] While I could provide countless examples of extreme market mispricing, a recent example stands out. In March 2009 investors were pricing in a higher probability of default in the triple-A rated debt of Berkshire Hathaway (run by Warren Buffett) than the dollar-denominated debt of Vietnam![12] This is simply ludicrous.

The important takeaway is that asset mispricing exists in markets. The implication of asset mispricing means that

---

[10] Graham, Benjamin; Dodd, David (2008) *Security Analysis: Sixth Edition.* New York: McGraw Hill
[11] Benartzi, Shlomo. (2008, December 1). Profiting From the Psychology of Investors. *The Financial Times.*
[12] Santoli, Michael. (2009, March 9). Where Pricing Anomalies Abound. *Barron's*, page 9.

there is not a single value for a security, but in fact there are actually two values for every security. There is (1) a market value and (2) an intrinsic value. However, this doesn't mean that every once in a while both values can't be equal.

A company's market value is equivalent to the firm's enterprise value, which is the combination of that firm's market capitalization (current market price of stock multiplied by shares outstanding) and net debt (long term debt less cash). This is simply the price offered on an exchange for the shares of that company at any given moment and is dictated by behaviors and emotions.

Conversely, the intrinsic value of a company is the price that someone would pay to buy the future cash flows that the firm can generate. Remember (because many forget) that when you are buying a stock, you are buying a percentage of the total business and the cash flows it can generate. If you could buy the whole company yourself or replicate its assets from scratch, how much would you pay? The answer is the firm's intrinsic value.

I am not suggesting that company fundamentals don't have a direct impact on share prices quoted on an exchange. But in the short term stocks will move around for many reasons, none of which have anything to do with the underlying value of that particular company. Benjamin Graham explains this phenomenon best by saying, "In the short run the market functions as a voting machine, and in the long run the market functions as a weighing machine."[13]

---

[13] Graham, Benjamin; Dodd, David (2008) *Security Analysis: Sixth Edition.* New York: McGraw Hill

Value Investing: A Disciplined Framework

Understanding that there is (1) a market value and (2) an intrinsic value is the first central tenant of value investing. Hopefully after reading the following paragraphs this concept should strike you as intuitive and obvious. A value investor takes advantage of the fact that human behavior governs market prices in the short-run, and occasionally:

You can purchase the shares of a corporation at a price quoted on a stock market that is at a significant discount to your estimate of that company's intrinsic value

In other words, would you be happy owning the business' cash flows for the current market price? As a value investor you goal is to buy $100 dollars of cash flows for less than $70. In practice, you would first determine a company's intrinsic value and then compare your estimate to the firm's stock price. If the market is valuing the company below its intrinsic value you should purchase the shares. As an aside, it is extremely important to remain independent and remove any opportunity of being biased by the market's opinion on valuation prior to reaching you own conclusion. Therefore, you should always calculate the intrinsic value before observing the market price.

After you buy the stock at a discount to your estimate of the company's intrinsic value you need to be patient and wait for the market price of the shares to increase to the point at which it matches your estimate of the intrinsic value. In the long-run, eventually both valuations will converge. It is critically important that you remain patient and keep the courage of your convictions. Do not expect the market to adjust immediately, as the market can plead temporary insanity for quite some time, and it may take months or possibly years for the stock to reach its intrinsic value. When the stock price eventually ascends to the intrinsic value you should sell the shares, take profits, and redeploy your capital in other undervalued investments.

However, be wary of being greedy. If you continue to hold the shares when they have exceeded their intrinsic value, then you are no longer investing, but rather speculating. Once the company's fundamentals can no longer justify a higher stock price, you are dependent on a greater fool's willingness to overpay. Even the best investors can be tempted to break this rule. For example; Warren Buffett knew that Coca-Cola was overpriced at forty times earnings and that those earnings were higher than normal because they were accomplished through financial engineering; yet he still did not sell his shares.[14]

While the market value is easily observable by simply looking up the most recent share price, the intrinsic value is an *estimate* and involves judgment (I will discuss the details of calculating a company's intrinsic value later in the value investing framework section). When you are estimating a company's intrinsic value it is imperative that you leave room for error, imprecision, and factors outside of your ability to predict, such as future economic output or unexpected demand shocks like the tragic events of September 11th. Therefore when you are measuring a firm's

---

[14] Schroeder, Alice (2008). *The Snowball: Warren Buffett and the Business of Life*. New York: Bantam Dell.

intrinsic value, you need to apply a range that should widen with uncertainty. An intrinsic value is never an exact number.

Understanding that your estimate of intrinsic value may be subject to misjudgment, it is important to protect yourself against the prospect of losing money if you are wrong and your estimate is too high. Every investment should have a meaningful buffer between the market price and intrinsic value. This leads us to the second central tenant of value investing:

You can minimize errors and increase the likelihood of earning a profit by buying stocks only when they are priced at a significant discount to your estimate of the company's intrinsic value, providing a "margin of safety"[15]

Investing with a margin of safety helps insure that you can earn substantial returns when you are right, and on the other hand minimize losses when you are wrong. For example, consider engineers building a bridge that must support 100 tons of traffic. Would the bridge be built to handle exactly 100 tons? Probably not. It would be much more prudent to build the bridge to handle more than 130 tons to ensure that the bridge will not collapse under a heavy load. The same can be done with securities. If you feel that a stock is worth $10, buying it at $7 will give you a margin of safety in case your analysis turns out to be incorrect and the stock is really

---

[15] Margin of safety is discussed at length by Ben Graham in his books *Security Analysis* and *Intelligent Investor*. Seth Klarman also expanded on the application of margin of safety in his book of the same title.

only worth \$9.[16] Essentially you are giving yourself some room for error if you overestimated the intrinsic value of the stock. By applying a margin of safety you are exposing yourself to the upside and handicapping your downside, tilting the odds of success in your favor.

Moreover, if your estimate of intrinsic value is correct, allowing for a margin of safety can lower the risk associated with an investment by providing you with a backstop against any considerable further weakness in share prices. While the market is clearly inefficient, it does have limits and once a stock moves significantly below its intrinsic value (say 50 percent), it becomes extremely difficult for that stock's price to fall much further as depressed prices will begin to attract investors.

For all intents and purposes you will always prefer an investment with the greatest margin of safety as calculated from the lower range of your estimate of intrinsic value. Therefore, the bigger the margin of safety; the lower the risk of the investment and the greater the potential financial reward.

Preservation of capital is very important for value investors. You should always spend considerable time understanding the risk of every investment, which is in effect how much money you can lose. Minimizing risk is one of the key benefits of requiring a margin of safety, as it can somewhat insure you against significant losses. As Warren Buffett

[16] This example was taken from the Investopedia website, who borrowed it from a similar example first used by Ben Graham or Warren Buffett. (http://www.investopedia.com/terms/m/marginofsafety.asp)

frequently opines when he lectures on the rules of value investing; "Rule #1 don't lose money. Rule #2: see rule #1".

However, please do not confuse risk with volatility. There is a significant push from the academic community and investment professionals to measure risk using volatility[17]. In fact, hedge funds have profited handsomely from this misconception. Hedge funds are favored by investment consultants because they can produce market-like returns with less volatility than the market. Yet they achieve this low volatility through the use of leverage! If the credit crisis of 2008 or failure of Long Term Capital Management a decade earlier has taught us anything; it is that leverage is very risky because it lowers the hurdle at which point you begin to lose money.[18] (I will further discuss the risks of investing with leverage later).

Using volatility as a measure of risk simply ignores common sense. Let me provide a couple of examples. First, suppose there are two stocks ("A" and "B") with similar businesses that are both currently priced at $50 per share. Then stock "A" increases to $90 per share and stock "B" falls to $10 per share. Given the change in prices, which stock is now riskier? If you use volatility as your measure of risk, then they are equally risky as the value of each stock has changed

---

[17] Volatility is measured as the standard deviation of the returns of financial assets over a specific time horizon. The greater the standard deviation, the greater the volatility, and theoretically the greater investment risk.

[18] For a good story about the use of leverage at hedge funds please see *"When Genius Failed"* by Roger Lowenstein, which chronicles the rise and fall of Long Term Capital Management. This hedge fund failed in 1998 and was found to be levered 25 to 1.

by equal absolute percentages. However given these price movements, if you measure risk based on how much money you can lose, then clearly stock "A" priced at $90 is far more risky than stock "B" priced at $10. Furthermore, does a U.S. treasury bond become riskier if the volatility of its market price increases? Of course not. A U.S. treasury bond is widely considered "risk free" because you will always be paid back, or in other words, you can't lose money in nominal terms. Bondholders don't focus on volatility, because they have learned from their position in the capital structure that risk should be measured by the probability of losing money. Equity investors would be wise to adopt a similar approach to measuring risk.

While always requiring an adequate margin of safety is an essential element to managing risk, you can further minimize the potential of suffering loses by only investing in companies whose businesses are rock solid and financially strong, thus allowing you to narrow the range of estimates when calculating their intrinsic value. Thus the third central tenant of value investing is:

Investing in quality businesses with strong balance sheets minimizes uncertainty and thus the risk of losing money or making significant errors in your estimate of intrinsic value.

Good companies are those with little or no debt and the capability of producing sustainable cash flows for the foreseeable future. Firms that have the ability to generate significant and growing free cash flows typically have a combination of strong barriers to entry, limited capital requirements, reliable customers, and low risk of technological obsolescence. These characteristics are referred to as economic "moats" and are tangible forms of ongoing competitive advantage, which is the key defense mechanism for maintaining cash flows in the face of competition.[19] Economic moats primarily come from four sources: (1) intangible assets such as brands and patents, (2) high switching cost for the customer, (3) network effects where it becomes an advantage of the product or service when more people use it, and (4) cost advantages that provide a permanent opportunity to sell at a lower cost than competitors.[20]

Essentially, you want to make sure that a company you invest in won't be out of business in 10 years. This is why it is better to invest in companies that have large moats such as utilities, ports, railroads or any other natural monopolies. You also want to avoid firms with high debt burdens, because if the economic environment deteriorates, leverage can kill even the best companies. Moreover, during times of market turbulence strong balance sheets can prop up share prices as the stock of firms with net cash positions (more cash than debt) will typically outperform similar companies that have moderate or heavier levels of debt. Strong balance sheets provide downside protection and are an additional mechanism to further reduce the risk associated with losing money on your investments.

---

[19] The term "economic moat" was first coined by Warren Buffett. An excellent description of the power of economic moats can be found in Roger Lowenstein's book, *"Buffett: the Making of an American Capitalist"*.
[20] Authers, John. (Undated). Revisiting Ideas behind True Value. *Financial Times*.

If you adopt a strategy of looking for stocks with wide moats and buying them when they're cheap, you shouldn't go wrong. Be wary of firms that rely solely on innovation or constant product improvements to sustain their competitive advantage.

When you combine all of the investing principles discussed above, you have the foundation that comprises the essential premise of value investing.

Value investing is the art of buying quality companies that generate sustainable and growing cash flows with strong balance sheets that have little or no leverage, whose shares trade at a significant margin of safety to your estimate of their intrinsic value.

Investing in quality businesses with regular cash flows, strong balance sheets, a good management team, and future prospects for defending those cash flows, combined with a margin of safety will more likely than not lead to strong investment returns.

Investors who have adopted this philosophy as the foundation of their investment strategy and remained true to its principles have produced long term returns that beat their respective market benchmarks. Below is a short collection of the investment strategies of a handful of renowned investors who have done the impossible and beaten the market. When you read each description please pay special attention to similarities in each method. Hopefully, each sounds familiar and a pattern emerges, as you should quickly realize that they are all describing the same system: value investing.

Warren Buffett of Berkshire Hathaway: "We seek to acquire great companies trading at a discount to their intrinsic value, and hold them for a long time. We will only invest in businesses that we understand, and always insist on a margin of safety. Regarding the types of businesses Berkshire likes to purchase; we want businesses to be one that we can understand; with favorable long-term prospects; operated by honest and competent people; and available at a very attractive price."[21]

Christopher Browne of Tweedy Browne: "The essence of [investing] is to buy businesses below their intrinsic value, giving yourself a big margin of safety. We're like bankers looking at loan collateral. We ask, what's the business worth? What have similar companies sold for? Does that price make sense? And can we buy the stock for a lot less? A stock that qualifies may take a week to rise to its true value, or five years, or it may never. But more often than not it does.[22]

Mohnish Pabrai of Pabrai Investment Funds: He values companies based on hard assets and cash flow, and only buys stocks when they are trading at half that value (50-cent dollars). His fund is also heavily concentrated in his best bets, typically owning only twelve companies. He does all his own independent research and doesn't talk to anybody

---

[21] I compiled Warren Buffett's philosophy from Berkshire Hathaway Annual Reports.
[22] Anonymous. (2008, January). The Prince of Value. *Money*, page 77.

about his stocks, as he doesn't want their views to cloud his judgment.[23]

Bruce Berkowitz of Fairholme: "I search for businesses with double digit free cash flow yields that won't dry up. We run a concentrated portfolio (just 22 stocks on $7.8 billion portfolio) and always maintain a healthy cash stake."[24]

Bill Miller of Legg Mason: He buys stocks he believes in and holds them for year (his funds turnover is around 13% making the average holding period of a stock 8 years). If he likes a stock at $40, he loves it even more at $30 and will continue to buy it as the price falls.[25]

Eddie Lampert of ESL Investments: He buys cheap stocks and holds them for long periods. He buys into companies whose assets he calculates are worth more than the current trading price. The idea is that he pays a price and great things may happen, but they don't have to happen for him to do okay. He also stays very concentrated and takes large positions in major companies and typically holds them for long times.[26]

Marty Whitman of Third Avenue: He invests in rock solid companies whose stocks are discounted at least 40% to his

[23] Bullock, Nicole. (2008, May). Looking Up to Buffett. *SmartMoney*, pages 77-79.
[24] Rosenberg, Yuval. (2008, December 22). When Bad Years Happen to Good Funds. *Fortune*, pages 81-84.
[25] Serwer, Andy. (2006, November 27). Will The Streak Be Unbroken?. *Fortune*, pages 213-222.
[26] Sellers, Patricia. (2006, February 20). The Best Investor of His Generation. *Fortune*, pages 90-104.

estimate of their intrinsic value, and that he believes have an ability to increase that intrinsic value by 10% or more annually. He keeps about 7% of his fund in cash, in part so that he doesn't have to unload shares at fire-sale prices for redemptions. Cheap or deep value is not a sufficient condition for investing; it has to be combined with creditworthiness (little to no debt).[27]

Ron Baron of Baron Capital: He focuses on small well-run companies that are the leaders in their industry that enjoy high barriers to entry. He wants firms that have a decent chance of doubling their earnings in 5 years without the use of leverage. He also only has 21% turnover in his fund (5-year average holding period) and concentrates money on his best ideas. He tells his analyst he doesn't want them thinking about the stock market, interest rates, or the economy. Instead he wants them on the phone with great companies, visiting them, or bringing them to visit us.[28]

Carl Icahn of Icahn Partners: He looks for companies that are screaming buys, meaning that the value of their assets far exceeds the total value of their shares. In general he looks for "hard assets" like real estate, oil reserves, and timberland that are relatively easy to value and resell, and avoids tech companies that depend heavily on developing new products. He'll buy at the worst possible moment, when there's no reason to see a sunny side and no one agrees with him. He explains: "the consensus is usually wrong. If you go with a

---

[27] Rosenberg, Yuval. (2008, December 22). When Bad Years Happen to Good Funds. *Fortune*, pages 81-84.
[28] Clash, James. (2008, October 27). Small Stocks, No Leverage. *Forbes*, pages 58-60.

trend, the momentum always falls apart. So I buy companies that are not glamorous and usually out of favor. It's even better if the whole industry is out of favor."[29]

Philip Tasho of Aston/Tamro: "Buy the best when they're depressed – like companies with little debt, and unique products and services. When the whole market sells down, focus on the higher-quality companies with experienced management."[30]

Mason Hawkins of Longleaf Partners: He hunts for industry leaders with clean balance sheets (little to no debt) and smart management teams whose stocks trade at discounts of 40% or more of their estimate of their true worth (intrinsic value). Their fund is highly concentrated and typically holds around 25 stocks.[31]

Bob Perkins of Perkins Investment Management: "If I make ten investments, three or four will be wrong. The trick is then not to lose too much money when you're wrong." He avoids blowups by buying stocks 10-15% off their lows and usually 60-80% off their highs. "If the stock is already off 50-80%, you've got to believe that a lot of the water has been taken out from it. That in itself minimizes the risk." He looks at the balance sheet for signs of strength, and then projects what a company can earn once it sorts its short term problems out (normalized earnings). He prefers minimal

---

[29] Tully, Shawn. (2007, June 11). Carl Icahn. *Fortune*, pages 117-124.
[30] Brandstrader, J.R. (2008, December 1). A Leader in His Pack. *Barron's*, pages 36-37.
[31] Rosenberg, Yuval. (2008, December 22). When Bad Years Happen to Good Funds. *Fortune*, pages 81-84.

amounts of debt, lots of cash, conservative accounting, excess cash flow, dividends or buybacks, and heavy insider-ownership and net buying.[32]

Scott Black of Delphi Management: He looks behind the numbers to find mispriced companies that offer super returns on equity, discounts to book or break up value, and other attractions not apparent in their shares. His favorites are low P/E stocks with high ROE's with sustainable earning power that generate substantial free cash flow and have strong balance sheets. He prefers negative net debt and a long history of ROE's north of 15%. Most picks appear to have earnings below 12x P/E. He also looks for companies trading below their breakup value. For example a Greek shipping company trading for $4 per share whose boats could be sold in market for $15 per share.[33]

Jim Kieffer and George Sertl of Artisan Partners: "We invest in companies that can generate sustainable earnings and cash flows in the future, and are financially strong with low debt levels, that trade at undemanding multiples and are out of favor with investors."[34]

David Winters of the Wintergreen Fund: He keeps a sizable cash cushion and holds his positions for the long term. He believes 5 years is a decent holding period, because good things happen to cheap stocks over a sweep of years not

[32] Franecki, David. (2001, March 26). Busted Stocks. *Barron's*, page F6.
[33] Rublin, Lauren. (2009, January 26). Barron's Roundtable: Good Thoughts. *Barron's*, pages 26-34.
[34] Taken from when Jim Kieffer and George Sertl were describing their investment process to a group of investment consultants.

weeks or months. He also believes that nobody can forecast stock prices, so the best thing to do is only buy with a large margin of safety.[35]

John Osterweis of Osterweis Funds: He hunts for out-of-favor names with strong cash flows and depressed valuations. He considers companies of any size or sector, but the goal is to focus on "value-like names that can be turned around, transformed, and made back into growth stocks." Usually 25% of his fund is in cash. He doles out cash when stocks suffer from any huge irrational liquidation.[36]

Susan Byrne of Westwood Holdings Group: "Our investment theme is buying high quality, low debt, dividend-paying companies that sell at less than the market multiple. The key is making sure in bear markets they don't go bust."[37]

Lee Ainslie of Maverick Capital: He first tries to understand as much as possible about the business. How sustainable is growth? How sustainable are returns on capital? How intelligently is the company deploying that capital? He values a company by comparing their estimate of sustainable free cash flow to enterprise value.[38]

---

[35] Grant, James. (2006, November 13). The Fat, Slow Pitch. *Forbes*, page 200.

[36] Rosenberg, Yuval. (2008, December 22). When Bad Years Happen to Good Funds. *Fortune*, pages 81-84.

[37] Colvin, Geoff. (2008, December 22). Stock Picks from the Experts. *Fortune*, pages 51-54.

[38] Dobbs, Richard. (2006, April). Inside A Hedge Fund: An Interview with the Managing Partner of Maverick Capital. *McKinsey Quarterly*.

Henry Sanders of River Road Asset Management: He uses an "absolute value" system to value stocks. He calculates absolute value through a combination based on what a business ought to be worth on the basis of free cash flow, and what he estimates the company would receive in a buyout. They then compare these numbers and give the number a conservative haircut, and only buy the stock if it is more than 15% below it. Sander's then creates a safety net by only investing in companies with big dividends (at least 2% yields) that don't cut in tough times and raise it over long periods. He also prefers companies with high insider ownership, little or no debt, and small or nonexistent Wall Street coverage.[39]

You will notice that many of these great investors focus on long investment horizons, holding cash, and independent thinking. These are mechanisms that they incorporated into their strategy to encourage discipline and rational thinking, which are necessary in order for value investing to truly be successful. After all if you plan on using the principles of value investing to exploit short term market inefficiencies, you must have the strength to avoid contributing to any inefficiency yourself.

---

[39] Bahree, Megha. (2008, November 10) Look For The Payout. Forbes, page 62.

Discipline Fundamentals and Human Behavior

Value investing is not just the ability to identify and invest in undervalued companies. It is the combination of this ability with a disciplined behavior, rational thinking, and control of your personal finances. You can only be successful at value investing if you have the financial wherewithal and self discipline to remain independent and unbiased so you can apply the value principles in a consistent manner over a long time horizon.

Being a disciplined investor begins with a clean balance sheet of your own. You should not start investing unless you have a sound financial foundation with no personal debt beyond a mortgage, car or student loans. Be cautious with credit cards and never carry a balance. If you have credit card debt now, pay off your balances before opening a brokerage account. You will never generate consistent investing returns above the typical double digit revolving rates that credit card companies charge.

As an investor it is critical that you live within your means and never spend more than you make. If you are investing with next month's rent check, you are speculating with money in an inefficient market and setting yourself up for failure. Only invest money that you can afford to lose and tie up for decades.

Furthermore, it would be prudent to wait until you've accumulated an emergency reserve fund of cash equal to at least six to twelve months of living expenses before you start investing. You need to give yourself the ability and the financial resources to survive the potential initial stock declines associated with buying out of favor value stocks. If you get forced to sell after stocks drop you are only guaranteeing the ability to buy high and sell low, and this is a loser's strategy.

If you have a solid financial foundation and are already investing, it is even more critical to exercise sound financial judgment in your investment portfolio to guarantee that you preserve capital and have the ability take advantage of depressed stock prices. As Warren Buffet explains; "You absolutely never want to be in a position where tomorrow morning you have to depend on the kindness of strangers in the financial world. Because you just can't be sure of anything. You have to think about things that have never happened before. You always want to have plenty of money around."[40]

To ensure that you never find yourself in a disadvantaged financial situation, it is essential that you adhere to two simple rules. First, it is critical to avoid leverage and never borrow to own stocks. Leveraging your portfolio is fun when times are good and things are on the way up. But leverage will destroy you on the way down. Irresponsible use of leverage has wiped out fortunes, caused hedge funds to implode, and brought international banks to their knees. Leverage simply has no place in the investment strategy of a long-term value investor.

Second, it is recommended that you hold meaningful levels of cash in you portfolio, say 10-25%. As you saw from the investing strategies of the experts above, it was common for many of them to hold significant cash positions so they can have some "dry powder" when the opportunities are best.[41] This is because when the market turns nasty and undervalued companies are easy picking, you will wish that you had more cash to put to work. Since World War II there have been thirteen bear markets, when stocks have fallen by twenty percent or more. Stocks rebounded an average of thirty four percent within a year of the end of these bear markets.[42] Be

---

[40] Schroeder, Alice (2008). *The Snowball: Warren Buffett and the Business of Life*. New York: Bantam Dell, page 823.
[41] Dry powder is a term used by money managers that is a reference to cash available to be immediately invested to take advantage of any sudden investing opportunities.
[42] Pearlman, Russell. (2009, January). Where to Invest 2009. *SmartMoney*, pages 49-59.

patient and hold cash so you can take advantage of bear markets when they come (roughly every 6 years). It is in the bear markets where opportunities to buy high quality companies will be best. Remember that markets are mean reverting. When bull markets begin expanded into their third year it is a good time to begin adding cash to your portfolio so you can load up when the inevitable downturn opportunity comes. Remember, in market upturns "trees do not grow to the sky", and in market downturns investors dump stocks regardless of their intrinsic value.

However, if you are running money for other people (particularly institutional investors) they may dislike the fact that you hold any cash. In his 2003 Baupost Year End Letter to Shareholders, Seth Klarman offers the best single explanation to ease clients concerns. He explains, "Perhaps some of our investors will soon be asking why you are paying us a management fee to hold so much cash. Let us preempt you by saying that you are not. You are paying us to decide when to hold onto cash and when to invest it, to determine when the expected return from a prospective investment justifies the risk involved and when it does not."[43] Holding cash and not having great uses for it can be painful, but not as painful as doing something stupid.[44] Holding cash also allows you to have a strict sell discipline, because you will never be forced to sell investments prematurely to fund shareholder redemptions.

---

[43] In 2003 the Baupost Group had roughly half of their assets in cash, and has always continued to hold large levels of cash.
[44] Warren Buffet's philosophy on holding cash: Schroeder, Alice (2008). *The Snowball: Warren Buffett and the Business of Life*. New York: Bantam Dell, page 792.

In addition to maintaining a strong financial position, it is important to be aware of complex issues associated with human behavior and the impact that powerful emotions such as fear and greed can have on your investment decision making process.

In order to profit from market mispricings it is essential that you remain unbiased and maintain a significant degree of independence. It is absolutely critical that you think for yourself and avoid the natural influence of herd mentality. It is extremely common for investors to get caught up in market euphoria or panic. It is difficult to sell when stocks are high and everyone is optimistic. It is even more difficult to buy at market bottoms when pessimism is widespread.

Individuals have a feeling that "someone knows something" and the market may be right, and then they start to second guess themselves. Economist Robert Shiller employs a social psychological explanation that he has termed "feedback loop theory of investor bubbles." Simply stated, the fact that so many people seem to be making big profits on the investment, and telling others about their good fortune, makes the investment seem too safe to pass up. More importantly, social pressure brought by having friends who are getting rich combined with the fear of missing out can be overwhelming to almost everyone but the most disciplined investor. Even if an investor identified the bubble and that the decision to proceed would be a very risky and thus foolish act, the investor is likely to proceed anyway if social and other situational pressures are strong.[45]

The best method for retaining your investing independence is to do all of your own homework on every investment, stay patient, and do everything possible to isolate yourself from popular opinion. Famed value investor John Templeton went as far as moving his office from New York City to the Bahamas to avoid the herd mentality on Wall Street. You need to think for yourself. If you depend on other people's views in financial matters (particularly Wall Street analysts and brokers) you will make lots of mistakes.

If you are practicing value investing, more often then not, you will be going against the crowd. After all, you are buying out of favor stocks. Successful stock picking means having the courage to take the contrarian market position. It's often the stocks with the most differing opinions that make the best investment opportunities. As Warren Buffet has lectured "you will pay dearly for a cheery consensus". The key to investing is to remember Ben Graham's credo, "Be fearful when others are greedy; and greedy when others are fearful."[46]

However, buying out of favor stocks usually involves purchases share in companies that have been falling precipitously and hitting new fifty two week trading lows daily. Many investors have difficulty buying these investments, because they are worried that the market can stay dysfunctional for a long time and prices may continue to

---

[45] Greenspan, Stephen. (2009, January 3). Why We Keep Falling for Financial Scams. *Wall Street Journal*.
[46] Famous advice of Ben Graham. Schroeder, Alice (2008). *The Snowball: Warren Buffett and the Business of Life*. New York: Bantam Dell, page 241.

fall. This is commonly referred to as "catching a falling knife". There is almost a compelling urge by investors to try to time the bottom, but all value investors know this is foolish, because in the short term markets are inefficient.

Everyone wishes they could identify when a stock will reach the bottom, but you have no idea, and either does anyone else. If someone claims they can forecast the bottom of the market, I suggest you run the other direction. Because anyone who believes they have this ability is engulfed with over-confidence, and there is nothing more deadly in investing then overconfidence and hubris. When you find a company that you believe is trading at a significant discount to your estimate (and remember it is an estimate not the exact value; re…overconfidence) don't wait for the perfect moment when the markets sink to their absolute floor.

Never hesitate to make an investment because you're not sure if it will fall farther in the immediate future. Inevitably, by the time you are certain that prices have reached a bottom, the opportunity will have passed and you will have most likely surrendered the lion share of the gains. In the vast majority of cases, its better to buy the stock early when you know it is cheap and suffer paper (unrealized) losses, versus the alternative of investing to late. Take the advice of Colin Symons of Symons Capital Management. "You can still buy low and sell high even if you can't time the bottom correctly. We have a good history of buying stocks awfully cheap and watching them go down 20%, but then they go up 100%. The key is to make sure the company can survive and return to normal earnings power. Look back historically to see how stressed out a company can get in a downturn and watch margins."[47]

Don't try to time the bottom or predict stock movements. Invest in assets when they are trading at a significant discount to their intrinsic value. At this point don't try to hold out for a bottom, you can't time it, so just invest now. The fact that businesses or the economy may get worse is not a good reason to avoid buying stocks at depressed prices.

Never try to predict stock prices. Just find great businesses at significant discounts to its potential cash flows, and hold over time. Repeat.

Moreover, it is perfectly acceptable to lose a few points while you continue researching an investment opportunity. It is more important to be thorough and avoid unforced errors. After all, as a long term investor, giving up a few points while you prove out your investment thesis is almost irrelevant. Never feel rushed.

Lastly, once you determine your investment principals, whether its value investing or not, it is important that you stick with those principals and never waiver, even at market extremes. If you loose your courage, give into the herd mentality, and change your strategy at market peaks and valleys, you will get crushed.

---

[47] Lambert, Emily. (2008, December 8). Catching the Hog Cycle. *Forbes*, page 132.

If you are ever feeling the pressure to abandon your principals or the urge to rush into an investment, take a step back and apply Warren Buffett's "Twenty Punches" approaches to making a disciplined investment decision: "You'd get very rich if you thought of yourself as having a card with only twenty punches in a lifetime, and every financial decision used up one punch. You'd resist the temptation to dabble, you'd make more good decisions and you'd make more big decisions."[48]

Achieving good returns in stocks requires taking a long term approach and remaining true to your disciplined investment strategy. Those who have self control over their emotions and can keep their focus and perspectives during trying times are more likely to emerge as successful value investors. You want to put yourself in the position where you will have the last laugh.

---

[48] Schroeder, Alice (2008). *The Snowball: Warren Buffett and the Business of Life*. New York: Bantam Dell, page 708.

Value Investing Framework

Hopefully, you now have a sound understanding of the benefits of a value-oriented investment strategy and the discipline required to give yourself the ability to succeed. It is time to apply the value investing principals described in detail above, and begin building a portfolio of companies trading at a discount to your estimate of intrinsic value.

Below is a framework of four steps that you should use for every investment. While it is important to always stay focused on the principals of value investing; these four steps offer insight into the actual mechanics necessary to execute the strategy. These steps should not appear complicated and should feel like an easy extension of the principals you have already learned.

As you will see, being a successful investor doesn't require complex formulas. It requires the combination of doing your own homework and rational thinking. Keeping your investment process simple is the easiest way to avoid falling victim to market fads, herd mentality, and your own overconfidence. In the end, you should understand what you are investing in and be comfortable with the company's business model and prospects for generating future cash flows. Stick to what you find simple, and if it's too difficult to quickly grasp, move on to other investments. When you are investing, remember that the goal of complexity in financial statements or investment vehicles is all too often to deceive, because most likely there is something to hide.

More importantly, like all other skills, successful investing takes practice. Like good wines, investors get better with age. Always learn from your experiences and review your process and decision making that lead to each investment you make. Learn from your mistakes and become a better investor.

1. Identify Companies with Moats:

The hardest part of investing is finding good investments. There are thousands of public companies whose common stock trades on American exchanges. Luckily, as a value investor you are searching for great companies that have economic moats. This naturally reduces the field to a few hundred prospects and is in fact a manageable task.

Your first step is to look for evidence that a company has an economic moat to begin with. In a capitalist economic system, companies that earn excess profits will draw competition and imitators. But companies with significant competitive advantages and economic moats can generate above average profits well into the future and are worth a whole lot more to investors.

You should look for evidence of economic moats in a company's financial statements. You should at least inspect the annual reports for the last five years and preferably ten. The fact that a company has a good year or two does not imply that they have a sustainable competitive advantage. They could be benefiting from a rising economy or a new product launch that hasn't drawn the attention of competitors yet. On the other hand, strong financial performance over the course of a decade is clearly an indication of an economic moat. Separately, observing how a company performs over an entire business cycle should give you a good indication of how the company executes in good times and bad, and will also help you determine normalized earnings when you value the company later.

Pat Dorsey, Director of Stock Analysis at Morningstar, uses the following financial metrics as hurdles to assist in determining the existence of an economic moat.[49] He calculates the average of each of the following four metrics listed below using a period of no less than five years.

1. Free cash flow margins greater than 5% (operating cash flow less capital expenditures divided by sales)
2. Net profit margins greater than 15% (net income divided by sales)
3. Return on equity over 15% (net income divided by stockholder's equity)

---

[49] Dorsey, Pat. (2004) *The Five Rules for Successful Stock Investing*. Hoboken, NJ: John Wiley & Sons, pages 22-24.

4. Return on assets over 6-7% (net income divided by assets)

Here is an example using Microsoft's financial statements.[50]

	1999	2000	2001	2002	2003	2004	2005	2006	2007	2008
Total Revenue	19,747	22,956	25,296	28,365	32,187	36,835	39,788	44,282	51,122	60,420
Gross Profit Margin %	85.7%	86.9%	86.3%	79.9%	81.2%	82.1%	84.8%	82.7%	79.1%	80.8%
Net Income Margin %	39.4%	41.0%	29.0%	18.9%	23.4%	22.2%	30.8%	28.5%	27.5%	29.3%
Cash from Operations	12,146	11,426	13,422	14,509	15,797	14,626	16,605	14,404	17,796	21,612
Capital Expenditure	(583)	(879)	(1,103)	(770)	(891)	(1,109)	(812)	(1,578)	(2,264)	(3,182)
Free Cash Flow	11,563	10,547	12,319	13,739	14,906	13,517	15,793	12,826	15,532	18,430
Free Cash Flow Margin %	58.6%	45.9%	48.7%	48.4%	46.3%	36.7%	39.7%	29.0%	30.4%	30.5%
Return on Assets %	20.5%	15.2%	13.2%	8.2%	8.0%	8.2%	12.8%	15.8%	17.9%	22.0%
Return on Capital %	27.8%	19.7%	16.5%	10.4%	10.2%	10.3%	17.2%	25.2%	33.4%	44.4%
Return on Equity %	34.6%	27.0%	17.4%	10.8%	12.9%	11.7%	19.9%	28.6%	39.5%	52.5%

A quick analysis of Microsoft's financial statements depicts a company that clearly has an economic moat. The ten year average for Microsoft's key financial metrics are: 25.5% free cash flow margin; 29.0% net profit margin; 25.5% return on equity; and 14.2% return on assets. Microsoft's financial performance clears Pat Dorsey's hurdles by significant margins. Hopefully none of these numbers appear as a surprise as Microsoft has long been the beneficiary of a virtual monopoly in the computer operating system software and office software markets.

While looking up old financial data is easy, determining if the company's economic moat will remain durable into the future takes more qualitative analysis and independent judgment. After all, you are buying the firm's future cash flows, not the money the company has already earned. As Warren Buffett jokes; "if past performance was any

---

[50] Data provided by Capital IQ.

guarantee of future performance the Forbes 400 would consist entirely of librarians."

The first place to begin when determining the sustainability of an economic moat is checking if there are any negative trends in the key financial metrics, as this may provide an early indication that competitors are making inroads into the company's business model. Observing Microsoft's financial trends, you can see that the profit margins and free cash flow margins have been trending slightly down, but at the same time return on assets and return on equity have been growing. From this analysis it appears that Microsoft's monopolies have held up well over time and demonstrate no meaningful evidence of deterioration.

Secondly, you should ask yourself if anything in their business model has changed which could cause them to lose their competitive advantage. For example, large pharmaceutical companies have generated economic moats via the government's protection of their patents on their drugs. Essentially their patents give the drug companies a virtual 20 year monopoly free from competition on any new drug they develop as long as it is unique.[51] However, if all of the pharmaceutical company's "blockbuster" drugs are going off-patent next year, and they do not have any new drugs in the pipeline, their economic moat will literally disappear overnight. Also check if there are new products, trends, or innovations on the horizon that could mitigate the company's moat. For example the newspaper industry used to be very profitable, as each major daily had a monopoly over their

---

[51] A patent in the United States has a 20 year life from its filing date.

local market. But with the rise of the internet, people can get their local news from many different sources besides the daily print edition.

Looking at Microsoft again, it is clear that their products have high switching cost and their competitive advantage should endure into the future. Their primary business is selling software to large corporations, and it is simply too expensive and risky for these customers to switch to an upstart software solution. An entire generation of office workers has been trained on Microsoft office software such as Word, Excel and PowerPoint. Any attempt to switch workers to a new unfamiliar software package would most likely be resisted by employees and result in lost worker productivity. Given this likely outcome it would take a transformational new product to justify and entice any switch from corporate customers.

Remember from the initial introduction to economic moats above, economic moats primarily come from four sources: (1) intangible assets such as brands and patents, (2) high switching cost for the customer, (3) network effects where it becomes an advantage of the product or service when more people use it, and (4) cost advantages that provide a permanent opportunity to sell at a lower cost than competitors.[52] If the company you are analyzing does not have one of these four types of structural advantages built into their business model, it is most likely that their advantage is not durable or sustainable.

---

[52] For more information and tools for analyzing corporate strategy and competitive advantage, I recommend Michael Porter's books on strategy.

2. Evaluate Financial Strength:

Evaluating a firm's financial strength is somewhat easier and more strait forward than analyzing the moat. There are really three tests to employ: (1) Is the firm levered, and if so, is debt a significant part of their capital structure, (2) If the firm does have debt, when does the debt mature, and (3) does the firm generate enough operating cash flows to cover their fixed costs and capital expenditure needs?

To analyze the level of leverage that a firm is employing, it is a good idea to begin with a look at the firm's net debt, which is calculated as their long term debt less any cash and cash equivalents. It is an excellent sign if the company has negative net debt, meaning they have more cash than debt. Thus if they needed to pay off their debt they could easily do so with cash on hand. It is even a better sign if the company has no debt and large stock pile of cash. For example, at Microsoft the firm has $2 billion in short term debt, but over $20 billion in cash on hand, resulting in negative $18 billion of net debt.

You can also use leverage ratios such as the debt to equity ratio and quick ratio. The debt to equity ratio is simply long-term debt divided by stock holder's equity on the balance sheet. The lower the number the better, and anything under 25% is considered conservative. The quick ratio is calculated by dividing cash on hand over current liabilities. This measures the ability of the company to pay off their short term obligations if they didn't take in another penny for the year. An excellent quick ratio would be considered anything greater than 100%. In the case of Microsoft, they have a debt to equity ratio of 6%, and a quick ratio of 85%.

If the firm does have debt you should also investigate when the debt is maturing and the bond's principal is due. The company will have to provide this information in their annual report. If the company you are investigating has debt that is maturing in the near future, they could be exposed to refinancing risk if credit markets are restricted as they were in the 2008 credit crisis. For example, if the firm doesn't have the cash to pay off the upcoming debt due, they could find themselves in distress and have to raise excess equity capital and diluting shareholders, which lowers the long term intrinsic value of each share. Naturally this is bad news for existing shareholders and will drive down the value of the stock. The further in the future any debt matures, the safer the stock. However, don't forget you can avoid this risk entirely by buying firms with little to no debt.

Lastly, you want to investigate how large the company's operating cash flows are in relation to their capital expenditure needs. It is important to understand how much capital the firm requires just to maintain their current operations. This is referred to as "maintenance capital". While some firms may not disclose their maintenance capital needs, the better ones will. You can find this information in the liquidity section of the company's annual report. The purpose of investigating this number is to make sure the company can continue investing in the business without having to raise new capital (debt or equity) if times get bad. A good test is to see how much operating cash flow the firm generated in their worst year of the last decade versus their needs for maintenance capital. For example at Microsoft, in their worst year since 1999 they generated at least $11 billion in operating cash flow, while the highest level of capital expenditures they have ever invested in a single year was only $3 billion. Operating cash flows would have to fall by more than seventy percent before they would need to worry about their ability to self fund investments of capital expenditures.

From this analysis of Microsoft's financial strength, the company is clearly in excellent financial condition. But it is important to remember that financial leverage can be beneficial to investor returns if it is used in *moderation* and the firm's operations are *relatively stable* and *non-cyclical*. However, be wary if a company has high leverage and is involved in a cyclical or volatile business or industry. Interest payments are a fixed expense and the company has to pay them whether business is good or bad. But a final word of caution, just because a company has shown stable operations through past business cycles doesn't guarantee that they can't be affected by future downward cycles. Each recession is different.

3. Estimate the Value of Shares:

There are really four methods that you can employ to determine the intrinsic value for the shares of a company. These methods are: (1) Normalized earnings approach; (2) Simple discounted cash flow approach; (3) Comparable transaction approach; and (4) Replacement value approach. Please note that these methods are intentionally meant to be moderately easy to employ. Many people feel that large complex Excel models are necessary to arrive at a descent valuation, but they all too often only increase the chance for poor estimates, formula errors, and overconfidence in the results. Moreover, it can take significant time to build complex models without adding significant value to your decision making process. Your time would be better spent evaluating the firm's business model and analyzing the durability of their moat.

The concept of using the normalized earnings approach to value a company is grounded in the recognition that a firm's earnings power should revert to the mean, and good times or bad times must eventually give way to a steady "normal state" over the life of the business cycle. By focusing on a firm's normalized earnings power you can hopefully avoid paying too much for a firm at the top of the business cycle when the business is firing on all cylinders, and on the opposite spectrum, shunning a stock whose industry may be temporarily weak.

To value a company using normalized earnings you need to first determine the normalized earnings per share for the business, and then multiply this number by a normalized price-to-earnings ratio that you would pay during "normal" market conditions for this company. This valuation technique can work especially well when analyzing companies that are out of favor or temporarily performing poorly. This is because when a company's near term prospects weaken, both earnings and the price-to-earnings multiple simultaneously contract. When things eventually turn around in a year or two, you benefit from the multiplicative effect of higher earnings and price-to-earnings multiples.

For example, let's assume that last year ABC Corp's earnings were $0.86 and you estimate that normalized earnings for ABC Corp are $1.00-$1.10. Due to ABC Corp's below average earnings performance, the stock's price-to-earnings multiple (which recall is awarded by an irrational market) has fallen from its long-term average (and in this example an appropriate normalized level) of 15x to a recent 9x. So the stock is trading at $7.74, which is equal to $0.86 multiplied by 9. To value the shares using normalized earnings you would multiply 15 by $1.00 and $1.10 to get a valuation range of $15 - $16.50 per share. This implies a margin of safety of approximately 48% and would be a good investment as long as you are comfortable with your estimation range of normalized earnings. As you can see, this valuation works well in cyclical industries as long as you have a long investment horizon.

To calculate normalized earnings for a company you start by computing the 10 year average net income margin and adjust net income for any extraordinary one time charges or losses. You then multiply this average adjusted income margin by the average annual revenue, assuming the firm is mature and no longer growing rapidly. Alternatively, if the company has been growing and you believe will continue to do so in the future, you may want to use the most recent annual revenue figure and give it a 10-20% haircut to be conservative. Of course, this computation can get more complicated if the firm has had several large acquisition or divestitures, or their revenue is correlated with a commodity that has fluctuated rapidly in the past, such as oil.

You then divide the normalized earnings figure by the current shares outstanding to reach the normalized earnings per share (as a note, you want to avoid just averaging the company's earnings per share over the last 10 years as shares outstanding could have fluctuated drastically over this time period). Lastly you multiply these normalized earnings per share estimates by a normalized price-to-earnings ratio to find the intrinsic value per share. When determining an appropriate normalized price-to-earnings multiple range, I would suggest never using more than 16x for growing companies or less than 10x for mature companies.

Let me continue using Microsoft as an example. Below I have calculated a value of Microsoft shares using the normalized earnings approach. I first adjusted the net income margin for any extraordinary items for the last 10 years. I then calculated a 10 year average adjusted net income margin which is 29.1%. Because Microsoft is still growing fast, I took the 2008 revenue of $60 billion and gave it a 20% haircut to be conservative. I multiplied this lower revenue number by the normalized adjusted income margin to find an estimate for normalized earnings ($14 billion). I then divided this number by Microsoft's shares outstanding (8.89 billion) to reach normalized earnings per share of $1.58. I then chose to use a normalized price-to-earnings ratio range of 14x-16x to account for the fact that Microsoft is an excellent company with good future growth prospects and a strong economic moat. I then multiply the normalized earnings per share with my estimate of an appropriate earnings multiple, which results in a valuation range of $22-$25 per share ($1.58 multiplied by 14 and 16). Including the value of Microsoft's cash per share of $2.28, I estimate the final valuation range for Microsoft's stock of $24-$28 per share.

	1999	2000	2001	2002	2003	2004	2005	2006	2007	10 Year 2008 Average
Total Revenue	19,747	22,956	25,296	28,365	32,187	36,835	39,788	44,282	51,122	60,420
Net Income Margin %	39.4%	41.0%	29.0%	18.9%	23.4%	22.2%	30.8%	28.5%	27.5%	29.3%
Extraordinary Items			1.5%							
Adjusted Margin %	39.4%	41.0%	30.5%	18.9%	23.4%	22.2%	30.8%	28.5%	27.5%	29.3% 29.1%

2008 Revenue	$60,420		Normalized P/E multiples		14x	16x
Conservative Haircut	20.0%		Normalized earnings		1.58	1.58
Normalized Revenue	$48,336		Share price		$22.19	$25.36
Normalized Margin	29.1%		Plus cash per share		$2.28	$2.28
Normalized Earnings	$14,089					
Shares Outstanding (MM)	8,890		Value of Microsoft		$24.47	$27.64
Normalized EPS	$ 1.58					

True intrinsic value is essentially the discounted value of all future cash flows available to shareholders, and thus using a simple discounted cash flow model is an excellent valuation technique. In fact, this method of valuation is preferred by many professionals and can include complex discounted cash flow models with an entire set of pro-forma financial statements many years into the future. However, as I have previously mentioned, these complex models require hundreds of estimates and formulas that are prone to error. These models also require investors to forecast entire financial statements line by line for three, four or five years into the future. The CFO of the company you are analyzing probably can't predict each line item that far into the future themselves, so what do you think the odds are that an outside investor could?

Valuing a company using the discounted cash flow method is slightly more complicated than the normalized earnings approach and involves more judgment. In this example I will keep things relatively simple and focus only on estimating future operating cash flows and capital expenditures. I start by using Microsoft's latest annual operating cash flows, and then I'll try to predict them out into the future to the point where the company reaches a normal growth state. To be conservative I gave the Microsoft's 2008 operating cash flow a twenty percent haircut and then held off on raising my estimates until 2011 to reflect a late economic recovery (hopefully the recession of 2008 and 2009 has ended by this time). I then grow operating cash flows by 3% annually after 2012 in line with the traditional long run economic growth rate.

Looking back over the last 10 years I estimated that annual maintenance capital expenditures are approximately $1 billion dollars. I then doubled this number to be conservative. I then subtracted capital expenditures from operating cash flow to reach an estimate of free cash flow for each year. I then attached a terminal value to my 2014 estimate of free cash flow.[53] I then discounted these free cash flows and terminal value by an annual compounded discount rate of 10%. I then added up all of these discounted cash flows to reach my estimate of net present value. Lastly, I subtracted the face value of debt outstanding and added back cash to reach the firm's intrinsic value. In this simple model of Microsoft's discounted cash flows I reached an estimated intrinsic value of $255 billion, or approximately $28 per share.

---

[53] For calculating the terminal value, I am using the Gordon Growth Rate Formula. This is equal to (2014 Operating cash flow * (1 + long term growth rate)) / (discount rate − long term growth rate). Using a discount rate of 10% and long term growth rate the formula would be ($19,186 * (1.03)) / (.10−.03) = $282,303.

	2008A	2009	2010	2011	2012	2013	2014	Terminal Value
Cash from Operations	$21,612	$17,290	$17,290	$19,019	$19,969	$20,569	$21,186	
		-20.0%	0.0%	10.0%	5.0%	3.0%	3.0%	
Capital Expenditure	-$3,182	-$2,000	-$2,000	-$2,000	-$2,000	-$2,000	-$2,000	
Free Cash Flow	$18,430	$15,289	$15,290	$17,019	$17,970	$18,569	$19,186	$282,303
Discounted Cash Flow		$14,578	$13,253	$13,410	$12,872	$12,092	$11,358	$159,353
Using 10% discount rate								

Net Present Value	$236,917
Less Debt	-$2,000
Plus Cash	$20,298
Enterprise Value	$255,215
Shares Outstanding (MM)	8,890
Value per Share	$28.71

The comparable transaction valuation methodology is most likely the simplest of all four valuation approaches. It involves uses various valuation metrics of companies that were sold in an acquisition or leveraged buy out. You then compare the valuation multiples paid by the acquiring form in the acquisition to calculate the value for your investment target. You are essentially estimating what your company would be worth if it was acquired or bought out in entirety. For example, you would find the average price to earnings multiple for the last 10 comparable transactions and then multiply that average ratio by the earnings per share of the stock you are analyzing. The primary challenge is finding data on comparable transactions.

It is difficult to find good comparable transaction examples for my example using Microsoft since the company is extremely large and a virtual monopoly. However, I will provide some fictitious transaction information to give you an idea of how comparable transactions value works.

As you can see below, there have been five transactions involving companies with similar businesses as Microsoft. I then calculated the transaction multiples using four standard valuation metrics (Price to earnings, Price to EBITDA, Price to book equity, and Price to revenue) that incorporate the value of the final purchase price for each company.[54] I then find the average purchase multiples for all five transactions and multiply these averages with Microsoft's financial metrics to reach an estimate of the purchase price that Microsoft would receive in an acquisition. The results of this analysis produce a valuation range between $25 and $32, with an average of $28 per share (remember this example is fictitious).

Name	Date	Value ($B)	Price to Earnings	Price to EBITDA	Price to Book Equity	Price to Sales
Company A	Jan-09	$55	14.3	11.0	8.3	12.4
Company B	Jul-08	$9	12.2	6.4	12.4	1.2
Company C	Jun-08	$5	18.0	5.7	9.5	1.8
Company D	Sep-07	$18	9.8	9.8	4.2	2.6
Company E	Apr-05	$22	13.1	11.5	7.1	3.2
Average			13.5	8.9	8.3	4.2

	Earnings	EBITDA	Book Value	Sales
Microsoft Financials	$17,232	$25,944	$34,478	$61,981
Average Multiples	13.5	8.9	8.3	4.2
Implied Value Using Multiples	$232,296	$229,984	$285,458	$259,232
Value per Share	$26.13	25.87	32.11	29.16
Average	$28.32			

---

[54] EBITDA is defined as Earnings before interest, tax, depreciation and amortization. This valuation metric is commonly used by the Private Equity industry. I highly advise that you avoid using this metric yourself when valuing a company because it omits many expenses, and is not a substitute for free cash flow. Jim Kieffer of Artisan Partners sarcastically refers to EBITDA as "Earnings Before I Think or Do Anything".

The last approach to valuation is using the replacement valuation technique. This is essentially estimating how much money it would take to replace all of the firm's physical and intangible assets. While this approach can be useful for business that rely on physical assets to generate the vast majority of their cash flows such as real estate investment trusts or truck leasing companies. It is extremely difficult to use for valuing intangible assets such as brand power or monopoly power. In the Microsoft example, the company's assets consist almost entirely of intellectual property and human capital, making is virtually impossible to estimate the firm's intrinsic value using the replacement value approach. I strongly recommend that you only use this method if you are extremely comfortable with determining the replacement cost of the company's physical assets. You should always try to stay within your circle of competence when making any investment decision, particularly surrounding calculating the firms valuation. The replacement value approach is best used as another data-point in determining your estimation for intrinsic value, and should not be exclusively relied on to calculate intrinsic value.

It is critical that you are comfortable with your calculation of valuation. If you value the company using two or more of these valuation approaches described above and reach similar conclusions, you should feel comfortable with you estimate. However, if you have a large range of values, you may take an average of every method and then just give this average a 10%-20% haircut for added conservatism. You should also demand a larger margin of safety or simply avoid the stock all together.

Moreover, never rely on relative trading multiples of similar firms for determining value. Because these relative metrics of valuation are subject to the whims of the market and are completely independent of the firms' true intrinsic values. You will commonly hear market pundits recommending a stock because it trades at a discount to its peers, however it would be unwise to act on this advice. This is because it is very rare that companies are identical enough to justify a true comparison. Even firms in the same industry can have drastically different business models, leverage, revenues, or profitability. Just consider Southwest's success in the otherwise disastrous airline industry. Similarly, it is virtually impossible to find companies with identical assets and liabilities.

The approaches described above should be more than adequate for the conservative value investor who always invests with a wide margin of safety. However, if you feel the need for more comprehensive education of valuation methodologies, please see Tom Copeland's book on the subject titled "Valuation: Measuring and Managing the Value of Companies". His book goes into the gory details of value creation and complex discounted cash flow modeling.

4. Wait for the Margin of Safety:

The last step in the value investing framework is waiting for the market to push the stock price to a significant discount to your estimate of the firm's intrinsic value. The price you pay for a stock is the most crucial step in this framework and should be chosen wisely. It is important to remain patient and only invest if you have a large margin of safety.

Value Investing: A Disciplined Framework

Although this step appears to be the simplest part of the framework, never underestimate the urge to make an investment before waiting for an appropriate margin of safety.

While there is no general consensus on the ideal margin of safety required before making an investment; on average shoot for a 30-40% margin of safety, and 25% for more stable great companies and 50% or greater for more speculative firms (which you shouldn't be investing in to begin with). Just remember, it is better to pay a fair price for a great company than a great price for a fair company.

I'll conclude the investment value framework by calculating the margin of safety using the Microsoft example. If you remember from above: I determined that Microsoft's conservative intrinsic value was $24-$28 per share using the normalized earnings approach, and approximately $28 using the simple discounted cash flow approach. Blending these estimates, it is fair to assume that $25-$28 is good approximation of Microsoft's intrinsic value. Microsoft's stock was most recently priced at $19 per share which represents a 24% margin of safety. Given the fact that Microsoft is an amazing business with good prospects and a substantial economic moat, I would probably consider investing in Microsoft if shares fell to less then $18 which would represent a margin of safety in excess of thirty percent. After all Microsoft was trading at $16 only a month ago. At $16 Microsoft is a steal, and an excellent value investment.

Additional Investing Topics

The key principals of value investing are captured above. In this section I hope to provide some additional insight on various topics that are important for every value investor to consider when crafting their investment strategy.

Dividends:

As a value investor, I recommend that you should be biased for companies that pay dividends, and require that a company have a meaningful dividend yield (say greater than 1%) as a final hurdle to help you determine if you want to add the stock to your portfolio or not.

Dividends are beneficial because they can provide a margin of safety in and of themselves. Dividend-issuing stocks are far less volatile due to their steady payouts, and usually outperform during market weakness. Companies that pay dividends tend to be stable, steady earners regardless of economic volatility. As I noted earlier when I was discussing financial strength; similar to strong balance sheets, dividends function sort of like anchors and help prop up stocks. While there's no guarantee their shares won't decline, a steady dividend payment can certainly mitigate losses.

In fact, research suggests that compounding dividends explains two thirds of total market returns over the long term.[55] This implies that over long periods, reinvested dividends contribute more to stock returns than rising share prices. For example, over the last two centuries ending in 2001, a $100 investment in US stocks grew to $37 million adjusted for inflation according to a 2002 study published by the Financial Analyst Journal. The average dividend yield of US stocks over this period was 4.9%. If dividends were pocketed and spent over the period instead of reinvested, that $100 dollars would have only grown to $2,099![56]

Dividends were also the principal driver behind the stock that had the best total return over the last 50 years among the stocks that comprise the Standard and Poor's 500 Index. Most investors probably assume that a fast-paced, innovative growth company would most likely take the title of best performing stock. However, between 1957 through 2006 the best performing stock in the Standard and Poor's 500 Index

[55] Lim, Paul. (2006, December 10). If You Cheer for the Tortoise, Applaud For Dividends. *New York Times*.
[56] Hough, Jack. (2009, January). All Hail The Dividend. *Smart Money*, pages 42-43.

was actually Philip Morris, (now known as Altria Group).[57] Many investors may be surprised to learn this fact given the bad news surrounding the firm over the last 20 years including strict government regulations and multi-billion dollar lawsuits. But the uncertainty and bad news surrounding Philip Morris allowed investors to reinvest their dividends (not to mention Philip Morris paid a generous dividend yield) in an out-of-favor and undervalued stock. In fact, $1,000 invested in Philip Morris in 1957 would have grown to $8.25 million by the end of 2006 if you continuously reinvested the dividends back into Philip Morris stock.[58]

Dividends also allow you to re-allocate capital versus management re-allocating it for you. If you can invest in undervalued companies using the value investing framework, you can re-allocate the money more effectively. The key assumption behind this intuition is that you have many more investment options and opportunities to reinvest dividends for a higher return then the company's management has if they reinvested the money internally.

Investors need to display a severe bias against big companies that don't pay dividends, no matter how glowing their growth rates are. CEO's will say there are more lucrative internal uses for cash than dividends, but research says otherwise. A study in 2003 found that since World War II, companies that paid the bulk of profit as dividends produced faster profit

[57] Siegel, Jeremy (2007) *Stocks for the Long Run: 4nd edition.* New York: McGraw-Hill, pages 59-61.
[58] Siegel, Jeremy (2007) *Stocks for the Long Run: 4nd edition.* New York: McGraw-Hill, pages 59-61.

growth over the following decade than companies that hoarded profit.[59] All managers talk about bright long-term prospects, but those who commit to paying shareholders dividends are more likely to deliver results. Dividends also help reduce management-agency issues and make the company more disciplined.

However, when analyzing dividend paying stocks, you want to look for stocks with a steady history of increasing their dividends, solid balance sheets and good prospects to keep the cash flowing to shareholders. For added safety, you want high dividend coverage ratios to make sure the company is generating enough cash to comfortably pay dividends and at the same time still invest in their business (capital expenditures).[60]

It is important to remember that reinvested dividends are more powerful than compounded interest (capital gains). Reinvested dividend payments beget more shares, and thus more dividend payments themselves, all in a glorious cycle as the company becomes more prosperous.

Stock Buybacks:

Some investors also look for share buybacks in the absence of dividends. Share repurchases have become more common

---

[59] Hough, Jack. (2009, January). All Hail The Dividend. *Smart Money*, pages 42-43.
[60] The dividend coverage ratio is measured by dividing the dividend by free cash flow. You ideally want to have a payout ratio below 50%. This way, operating cash flow could fall by half and the company could still invest in capital expenditures and pay the dividend.

since the increase in employee stock options for executive compensation.[61] However, unlike dividends, share repurchases can create or destroy shareholder value.

Stock buybacks can create value if management is selectively repurchasing shares when they think their stock is undervalued. The market often rewards companies with share repurchases because they shrink shares outstanding, thus reducing the denominator in earnings per share. The new higher earnings per share figure increases the value of stock as long as the price-to-earnings ratio awarded by the market remains constant. The market typically rewards bigger repurchases, but ironically many investors favor long-term regular buying versus the irregular buying only when cheap. It is important to check and see that management is only repurchasing shares when they think that the company's stock price is too low and shares are undervalued.

However, all too often buybacks destroy shareholder value because companies tend to repurchase more shares during the good economic times when their stock is expensive and probably overpriced. Separately, buybacks can also be a cover for management teams that are exercising options (this is probably more the rule than the exception). Two separate studies by Georgetown University and Birinyi Associates both found that companies that announced share repurchases surprisingly had the number of shares actually *increase* by

---

[61] Corporate executives compensated with stock options will push for stock repurchases instead of dividends. This is because dividends reduce the value of their options while share repurchases increase the value of their options. Be wary of the intentions of any management team with lots of stock options pushing share repurchases over dividends.

24-33%![62] It is important to observe that buybacks are actually reducing shares outstanding over many years. If not, the company management is buying back expensive shares enrich themselves through stock options at the expense of stock holders. You should consider this tantamount to theft and avoid the company.

Diversification:

"People say the whole secret of investing is diversification, but this idea is ass-backwards!"
- Charlie Munger[63]

It is important to diversify, but never forget that most wealth in the United States was created through the concentration of assets. Many professionals strongly believe that an undiversified portfolio is risky. I concede that a portfolio of ten stocks is extremely risky in the short term. However, a disciplined investor using the value investing framework who always uses common sense, does their homework, invests in their circle of competence, and always applies a significant margin of safety should be able to hold a concentrated portfolio of twenty to thirty stocks with a low level of risk.

If you are going to beat the market, you can't hold so many stocks that you mimic the market. Moreover, if you are closely adhering to the value investment framework, there may not be an opportunity to invest in forty great ideas.

---

[62] Rehfeld, Barry. (2006, December 3). At The Buyback Mall, It Pays To Shop Around. *New York Times*.
[63] Machan, Dyan. (2008, September). Buffett's Best Man. *SmartMoney*, pages 83-85.

Many of the greatest investors such as Warren Buffett, Eddie Lampert and Mohnish Pabrai load up on only their best investment ideas, essentially making big bets on the handful of businesses that can be winners. During several times in the beginning of his career, Warren Buffett held single stock positions that comprised more than half his portfolio.[64]

Avoiding Value Traps:

The major risk of being a value investor and seeking companies that are out of favor with the market, is that this practice can result with an investor being snared in a "value trap".

Bill Miller of Legg Mason Value Trust provided the following description of value traps to Fortune Magazine in 2006: "Value traps tend to have certain characteristics. Typically, one is the valuation of the business or industry is lower than its historical norms. The company normally has a fairly long history, so the historical normal valuations provide a lot of comfort. Therefore, when you get down towards the lower end of these valuations, value people find them attractive. The trap comes in when there's a secular change, where the fundamental economics of the business are changing or the industry is changing, and the market is slowly incorporating it into the stock price. So that would be the case over the last several years with the Newspaper industry. They are a good example of where historical valuation metrics aren't working."[65]

---

[64] Schroeder, Alice (2008). *The Snowball: Warren Buffett and the Business of Life*. New York: Bantam Dell

[65] Serwer, Andy. (2006, November 27). Will The Streak Be Unbroken?.

Choosing companies that are experiencing unfavorable conditions or a downturn in their business cycle may be good investments, but you must analyze their ability to stay solvent. As I discussed in the financial strength section of the value investing framework; companies with too much debt may not have the ability to make interest or principal payments and survive in difficult economic environments. One of the keys in identifying cheap stocks is making sure the can generate enough cash flows to pay the bondholders. This is why it is advantageous to focus on companies that have low or no debt so they are never pressured to do stupid things when they face financial adversity; like filing for chapter eleven bankruptcy.

Strategies for avoiding value traps:
1. Check if the basic business model is evaporating or imploding (e.g. Newspapers). Make sure the nature of the business hasn't changed and ask yourself, "Does the business model still work?"
2. Make sure the company is generating enough cash to cover debt liabilities and capital spending requirements. Double check the firms leverage ratios.
3. Think independently, and avoid what other people are saying.
4. If story is too good to be true, it usually is.

Investing in Financials:

In my opinion, banks should never be perceived as high quality. They depend on leverage and can get killed in difficult and uncertain economic periods. Over the course of five to ten years financials can have high stable returns. However, every ten to fifteen years the market forces half of the financial sector into bankruptcy or very close. Severe financial crises are becoming cyclical as they are occurring frequency almost once a decade. Using Citibank as an example: the bank's stock regularly looses 75% of its market value once a decade like clockwork. Fortunately, this economic beating only appears to happen regularly with financial stocks.

Moreover, you should avoid financials because you can't value their assets and thus their stock. Until the day when banks and broker/dealers open their books to the public every quarter, you just don't know what you're buying. Additionally, many financial stocks are subject to significant counter party arrangements and risks. Therefor their value is often a function of the quality of their reputations and the solvency of their counterparties. A good reputation can vanish overnight and doesn't constitute an economic moat. I give you Bear Stearns and Lehman Brothers as case in point.

Top's Down vs. Bottom's Up Investing:

Investing magazines and commentators often refer to top's down or bottom's up investing styles. Top's down is when investors judge where the market and overall economy is headed and then try to choose the sectors that they believe will outperform. This needless to say is extremely difficult. After all Nobel winning economist can't seem to predict the business cycle even though they have access to reams of economic data and research assistants to crunch numbers. If they can't do it, how can the ordinary investor? Predicting which sectors will outperform can be even more difficult, as even this analysis takes hundreds of inputs and extensive models which only lead to tremendous opportunities for error.

Conversely, bottom's up stock picking means finding individual companies that are undervalued and have strong business prospects. This of course drastically decreases the needed analysis and potential input, and represents a far simpler task that is realistically achievable by an individual investor. Also the risk of errors in estimates of undervaluation and future performance can be drastically reduced at the individual stock level through applying a margin of safety in you analysis (which in itself acknowledges that you are only human and bound to make mistakes).

Conclusion

I hope you have found the principals of value investing an enlightening and logical strategy for investing. Most of the information should have struck you as common sense and sound judgment, which you can easily apply in your own portfolio. The key to successful investing is persistently staying disciplined and employing the value investing framework before you make any investment decision, thus ensuring that you don't lose your independence or fall victim to Wall Street's herd mentality, rushing haphazardly into the latest hot stock tip. Always methodically and thoroughly complete each step of the value investing framework:

1. Identify companies with moats
2. Evaluate financial strength
3. Estimate the value of shares
4. Wait for the margin of safety

Value Investing: A Disciplined Framework

Remember to take a long term approach when investing. Avoid constantly monitoring your portfolio's every move, as the thrill and excitement of the market can easily overwhelm the instincts of even the most disciplined investor. Hesitation is often the best response to any sudden impulse to invest. Time is your friend. Always review your process for each investment and try your best to learn from your successes *and mistakes*.

Finally, two important aspects of being a successful investor are a passion for studying business and continuously expanding your investing skills and knowledge. You should regularly read investing and business books or articles to further expand your circle of competence. Many great investors have written books and articles discussing their investing experiences and sharing their market knowledge. I will leave you with a list of books that I have found helpful as a value investor.

Security Analysis; Sixth Edition – Benjamin Graham and David Dodd

Intelligent Investor – Benjamin Graham

Common Stocks for Uncommon Profits – Philip Fisher

Value Investing: From Graham to Buffett and Beyond – Bruce Greenwald
Value Investing: A Balanced Approach – Marty Whitman

Five Rules for Successful Stock Investing – Pat Dorsey

Value Investing: A Disciplined Framework

Margin of Safety – Seth Klarman

The Essential Buffett – Robert Hagstrom

The Warren Buffet Way – Robert Hagstrom

The Dhandho Investor - Mohnish Pabrai

The Little Book of Value Investing – Christopher Browne

The Little Book that Beats the Market – Joel Greenblatt

Stocks for the Long Run – Jeremy Siegel

Buffett: The Making of an American Capitalist – Roger Lowenstein

Value Investing Framework in Action

Below are three research reports that utilize the concepts of the value investing framework. Please use these reports as examples of the minimum necessary steps you should take before making any investment decisions.

Rockwell Automation (ROK)

Executive Summary:

In my opinion Rockwell Automation (ROK) is an attractive
investment target. ROK is well positioned to continue
generating strong, sustainable cash flows in an industry with
excellent long term prospects as manufacturing becomes
more automated. Although the near term may be cyclically
weak, I think it is unreasonable to assume manufactures
won't continue automating facilities as it is essential to
sustain competitiveness. The company has a strong balance
sheet and is trading at irrationally low valuations. At $25.71
per share, ROK is currently trading at a 45% margin of safety
to my estimate of intrinsic value of $46-$60 per share. ROK

is trading at a forward P/E of 6.3x (Street estimate of $4.09 per share), and an implied P/E of 7.9x-6.9x based on my estimate of normalized earnings ($3.25 - $3.75 per share). I believe a 14-16x P/E multiple may be appropriate given the long term growth prospects of the manufacturing automation industry and ROK's plans for future acquisitions and stock buybacks. Over the last 10 years earnings grew in excess of 20% every year but 2001.

Company Overview:

ROK provides industrial automation, power, control, and information solutions for capital intensive and complex manufacturing as well as distribution systems for warehousing. The company has operations in North America (58% of sales), Europe, Middle East and Africa (23%), Asia-Pacific (12%) and Latin America (7%). The primary end markets served by ROK include: Consumer/Medical (42% of sales), Infrastructure (31%), Auto (14%), Industrial (10%), and Government (3%). Below are key financial results of the business over the last 10 years.

Year Edning Sep 30	1998	1999	2000	2001	2002	2003	2004	2005	2006	2007	2008	10 year Average
Total Revenue	$6,834	$4,699	$4,661	$4,285	$3,776	$3,992	$4,411	$4,112	$4,556	$5,004	$5,698	$4,730
Gross Margin %	23.8%	32.5%	33.3%	30.3%	31.4%	32.8%	35.4%	40.5%	41.7%	41.9%	41.1%	35.0%
Net Income Margin %	(6.2%)	11.9%	13.6%	7.1%	3.2%	7.2%	9.4%	13.1%	13.3%	29.7%	10.1%	10.2%
Cash from Ops.	$551	$812	$704	($14	$437	$436	$624	$665	$424	$459	$591	$517
Capital Expenditure	($408)	($250)	($217)	($157)	($100)	($108)	($98)	($103)	($122)	($131)	($151)	($168)
Free Cash Flow	$143	$562	$487	($171)	$337	$329	$526	$562	$302	$328	$440	$349
Free Cash Flow Margin %	2.1%	12.0%	10.4%	(4.0%)	8.9%	8.2%	11.9%	13.7%	6.6%	6.6%	7.7%	7.7%
Return on Assets %	1.5%	4.6%	5.4%	4.0%	4.3%	5.4%	7.7%	9.5%	10.2%	11.3%	12.4%	7.0%
Return on Capital %	2.4%	8.0%	8.9%	6.1%	6.9%	8.8%	12.7%	16.6%	18.0%	18.9%	21.1%	11.7%
Return on Equity %	(2.7%)	9.8%	13.2%	5.9%	13.9%	17.6%	20.5%	25.5%	29.7%	31.1%	33.7%	18.0%

ROK operates two segments: Control Products & Solutions Segment (57% of sales) and Architecture & Software Segment (43% of sales). The Architecture & Software segment includes various elements of its integrated control and information architecture capable of connecting the customer's entire manufacturing system including real time information software that can manage and monitor plant-wide information systems.

The Control Products & Solutions segment combines a portfolio of motor control and industrial control products with the customer support and application knowledge necessary to implement an automation or information solution on the plant floor. This segment also offers services designed to help improve a customer's automation investment and provide life-cycle support, including multi-vendor customer technical support and repair, asset management, training and predictive and preventative maintenance.

Industry & Competitive Position:

ROK is the leader in discrete manufacturing automation and enterprise manufacturing intelligence and services industry. They have established a strong competitive position in the automation industry as a result of their complete scope of plant floor products, leading technology platform, large installed base, established global distribution network, and reputation for quality. Their competitors are either (1) large conglomerates who at times aren't as competitive due to their large bureaucracies, or (2) smaller competitors who only serve smaller niches. ROK has the advantage of a complete product portfolio, which has increased their win rate as procurement and operations managers prefer one-stop-shopping.

The Architecture & Software segment competitors include: Siemens, Emerson Electric, Mitsubishi, Omron and Schneider Electric. The Control Products & Solutions segment competitors include: General Electric, ABB, Emerson Electric, Honeywell, Siemens, Eaton, Invensys, and Schneider Electric.

Economics & Strategy:

ROK has a 3 prong strategy that in my opinion has produced successful results, and I see no reason why maintaining this strategy shouldn't continue to be successful. Their strategy includes; (1) expanding globally to manufacturing plants in emerging economies who are comprising a larger portion of the global manufacturing capacity; (2) expanding automation to new industries including life sciences, oil and gas production, and mining; and (3) offering services beyond automation including process control, safety controls, and information management [Enterprise Manufacturing Intelligence Software]. This strategy will continue to boost organic growth, diversify their business, and increase their addressable markets.

ROK's goal is to build the capability to construct the entire plant floor including machinery, distribution, safety, and information management. The company has been building out their safety ($3 billion market growing 10%) and information management ($3 billion market growing 12%) products through a combination of R&D and bolt on acquisitions. They believe they have the capability to earn a larger share of new factory contracts and have subsequently been adding information services to existing customer's platforms. They have also grown in the resource end market (including energy, mining and industrials), and are now more diversified across both the consumer OEMs and the resource end markets.

In the future, the company will continue to focus on global growth as manufacturing moves from developed countries to emerging markets. ROK's sales to Latin America, EMEA and Asia-Pacific have all been growing greater than 25% annually. The company also plans to continue growing through small bolt-on acquisitions that they can attach to their current platform. The company can then quickly increase the acquired firm's revenues by selling the product through their global customer base.

In September the company announced it would be restructuring operations in anticipation of a negative capital spending cycle, resulting in a $50 million pretax charge (-$0.25 EPS). ROK expects to generate cost savings of approximately $75 million in fiscal 2009, growing to $85 million in fiscal 2010.

Controversy:

A.   The process automation industry is highly cyclical and the recent manufacturing slowdown over the last several months has hurt ROK's near term prospects. Potential customers' are struggling with (1) a lack of access to financing; and (2) unexpected excess capacity from a decrease in demand, both of which have curtailed planned capital spending. According to the Federal Reserve manufacturing capacity utilization in the U.S. has fallen over the last year from 80% to 76%. Manufacturing capital investments typically falls when capacity utilization is below 79% and rises when above 79%. U.S. customers account for 51% of ROK's sales.

B.   Most of ROK's growth has been coming from emerging market expansion. However, emerging market economies are slowing faster then expected and may take longer to recover than domestic economies. At the same time international profit growth has benefited from a weak dollar. As the dollar strengthens international profits will be adversely impacted.

C.   ROK has traditionally used commercial paper for short term financing. Last reported, ROK had $320 million of commercial paper outstanding with an average maturity of 5 days. However, the company has the ability to repay commercial paper and continue funding short-term needs through excess cash on hand ($761 million) and unused credit facilities ($600 million available, expiring Oct 2009). Separately, no long-term debt principal is payable before 2017. It is absolutely critical to the firm's business model that they appear financially strong, as manufactures won't do business with an automation company if they are worried about the future health of ROK.

Reason to Own:

A.   While the current manufacturing slowdown and weak global economy may hurt ROK's near term prospects, in the long term more companies will need to automate manufacturing and distribution facilities to lower labor costs, improve worker safety, and effectively compete in the global economy. Companies must automate manufacturing to generate and retain a competitive advantage.

B.   The company has a good history returning excess cash to shareholders. ROK has a 4% dividend yield. In the first 9 months of Fiscal 2008, ROK repurchased 4.3 million shares for $251.7 million for an average of $58 per share or 2.9% of shares outstanding. As of June 30th ROK still had board authority to repurchase $775 million in stock, roughly 30 million shares at today's stock price or 21% of shares outstanding.

C.   The automation industry is highly competitive. Relatively speaking, ROK is a small company considering many of their competitors are conglomerates. Nevertheless ROK has held share and been successful winning new contracts. At current valuations, I think there is an above average chance that ROK could be acquired by one its larger competitors once credit markets loosen.

Valuation:

ROK currently trades at $25.71 per share which equates to a trailing P/E multiple of 6.3x and a forward ratio of 6.3x. Normalized earnings are difficult to measure as the company has acquired several businesses over the last several years and divested large non-core business units. Adjusting for acquisitions, divestitures, and share repurchases I believe normalized earnings are in the range of $3.25 - $3.75 per share, not including future acquisitions or share buybacks.

Management's EPS guidance is $4.00-$4.10 per share in 2008. Wall Street is forecasting $4.09 per share for fiscal 2009 with a high estimate of $5.05 and a low estimate of $3.40.

Normal Revenue ($B)	$4,730	$4,730
Normal Income Margin	10.2%	10.2%
Normalized Earnings	$484	$484
P/E Multiple	14	16
Estimated Value	$6,775	$7,743
Shares Outstanding (MM)	141.78	141.78
Value per Share	$47.79	$54.61
Cash per Sahre	$3.91	$3.91
Total Value per Share	**$51.70**	**$58.52**

I believe the long term growth prospects for ROK are bright and a 14-16x P/E multiple is warranted. Using my normalized EPS estimates of $3.25 - $3.75 per share, I believe the intrinsic value of ROK is between $46 and $60 per share. This represents a 45% margin of safety. Additionally, ROK currently has a 4% dividend yield which will boost returns.

Financial Strength:

ROK is financially sound with good operating leverage (16% operating margins and 11% net profit margins) and strong cash flow (average free cash flow for last three years of $316 million). ROK has $463 million in net debt comprised of $761 million in cash, $320 in commercial paper, and $904 million in long term debt (that begins to expire in 2017). The company has an additional $600 million unused credit facilities. The company has ample cash to continue paying off its commercial paper and fund its $170 million annual dividend and any additional share repurchases. The debt to EBITDA ratio is 1.1x. The company has an A credit rating with stable outlook.

I believe ROK will continue to remain financially strong as management understands it is extremely important to the firm's business model, as their customers will only do business with financially sound firms that will be around to service contracts.

Diamond Offshore (DO)

Exec Summary:

Diamond Offshore Drilling (DO) is trading at $69 representing a market capitalization of $9.6 billion and a 10.2% dividend yield (the yield is very high because the company pays out all excess cash as a special dividend). DO has generated a 10 year average ROIC of 17.5%, approximately double their cost of capital. In my opinion, DO should be able to generate FCF in the range of $500-$1,100 million annually for the next several years. The company is in excellent financial condition with a net cash position of $237 million ($740 in cash and $503 in debt), no debt maturing until 2014, and a $10.3 billion contract backlog (equivalent to 3 years of revenues). DO is currently trading at a 25% discount to my estimate of intrinsic value which is around $75-$95 per share. The company is extremely shareholder friendly and is 50% owned by Loews Corp.

I would recommend that an investor require at least a 30% - 40% margin of safety if investing in DO because of the firm's correlation with volatile oil prices and the value of the dollar. If the stock trades down to $45-$53, I believe it would represent a superb opportunity to invest in an excellent business at a fair discount to its intrinsic value.

Company Overview:

DO is a global owner and operator of offshore oil and gas drilling platforms (rigs). The company provides offshore drilling services with capabilities deep water, shallow water, and harsh environments for independent and government-owned oil and gas companies. DO operates highly specialized deep-sea semisubmersibles, conventional semisubmersibles, and shallow water jack-ups. As of December 31, 2008, DO operated a fleet of 45 offshore rigs comprising 30 semisubmersibles (of which 11 are high specification deep-sea), 14 jack-ups, and 1 drill ship. The company was founded in 1989 and is headquartered in Houston, Texas. DO operates as a subsidiary of Loews Corporation. Below is a summary of the company's outstanding financial results for the last 12 years.

	1997	1998	1999	2000	2001	2002	2003	2004	2005	2006	2007	2008
Revenue	$956.1	$1,208.8	$821.0	$684.5	$924.3	$752.6	$680.9	$814.7	$1,221.0	$2,052.6	$2,567.7	$3,544.1
Gross Margin %	57.5%	59.9%	47.4%	33.1%	45.5%	34.3%	24.5%	26.7%	44.8%	57.6%	58.6%	64.7%
SG&A Margin %	2.4%	2.1%	2.8%	3.5%	2.8%	3.9%	4.2%	4.0%	3.0%	2.0%	2.1%	1.7%
Net Income Margin %	29.1%	31.7%	13.0%	10.6%	18.8%	8.3%	(7.1%)	(0.9%)	21.3%	34.4%	33.0%	37.0%
Diluted EPS	$1.93	$2.66	$1.11	$0.53	$1.26	$0.47	($0.37)	($0.06)	$1.91	$5.12	$6.12	$9.43
Cash from Ops.	$396.4	$547.2	$398.1	$196.5	$370.7	$288.6	$162.5	$208.3	$388.6	$760.1	$1,208.3	$1,619.7
Capital Expenditure	($362.6)	($224.5)	($324.1)	($323.9)	($268.6)	($340.8)	($272.0)	($89.2)	($293.8)	($551.2)	($647.1)	($666.9)
Free Cash Flow	$33.8	$322.7	$74.0	($127.4)	$102.1	($52.2)	($109.6)	$119.1	$94.7	$208.9	$561.2	$952.8
Common Dividends	($19.5)	($69.2)	($67.9)	($67.6)	($66.5)	($65.7)	($57.0)	($32.3)	($48.3)	($258.2)	($69.3)	($69.5)
Special Dividend	$0.0	$0.0	$0.0	$0.0	$0.0	$0.0	$0.0	$0.0	$0.0	$0.0	($727.0)	($782.7)
Total Dividends	($19.5)	($69.2)	($67.9)	($67.6)	($66.5)	($65.7)	($57.0)	($32.3)	($48.3)	($258.2)	($796.3)	($852.2)
Cash & ST Invest	$466.1	$637.0	$641.4	$862.1	$1,147.4	$810.1	$610.3	$927.9	$844.9	$827.3	$641.6	$740.5
Long-Term Debt	$400.0	$400.0	$400.0	$856.6	$920.6	$924.5	$928.0	$709.4	$977.7	$964.3	$503.1	$503.3
Net Debt	($66.1)	($237.0)	($241.4)	($5.6)	($226.7)	$114.4	$317.7	($218.4)	$132.8	$137.0	($138.5)	($237.2)
Return on Assets %	13.5%	14.5%	5.3%	1.2%	4.3%	1.0%	(0.6%)	0.1%	5.8%	15.2%	17.9%	25.8%
Return on Capital %	16.3%	17.4%	6.4%	1.5%	5.0%	1.1%	(0.7%)	0.1%	7.2%	19.2%	22.8%	33.1%
Return on Equity %	20.4%	23.3%	8.7%	4.0%	9.6%	3.4%	(2.8%)	(0.4%)	15.0%	33.9%	32.6%	42.1%

Industry & Competitive Position:

The off shore drilling industry is separated into two categories, shallow and floater (mid and deep sea). The shallow drilling is performed by jack-up rigs that operate in up to 400 feet of water. The vast majority of ocean rigs are jack-up rigs as they are (1) easy to deploy in shallow water, (2) cost around $125 million, significantly less than Deep Sea rigs, and (3) most of offshore oil exploration had traditionally been in shallow water due to technology constraints and low exploration costs. This jack-up market has been very volatile with the run up and subsequent decrease in oil and natural gas prices. Oil companies have let jack-up rig contracts expire and there is currently an oversupply of rigs (particularly in the Gulf of Mexico), and there is uncertainty surrounding future leases and day rates. Current day rates for jack-ups are between $120-$140K and have daily cost around $45K.

The deep sea or "floater" segment is comprised of semisubmersible rigs and drill-ships that operate in water depths of greater than 2,000 feet and up to 10,000 feet. The market for rigs that can drill in excess of 4,000 feet are still performing well, and lease rates in excess of 7,500 feet are the strongest. The average day rate for deep sea highly specialized rigs is between $500-650K per day and costs of approximately $100K per day providing operating margins north of 75%. Demand for the floater market has remained strong in the face of falling crude prices and DO estimates that the economic floor for profitable deep-sea drilling is around of $50 per barrel. These contracts are longer in duration and are usually for 2-5 years. Furthermore, the demand for these rigs should remain strong as the majority of future off-shore exploration efforts will be in deep water, and the majority of new oil reserves discoveries have been found in deep water (Brazil, Gulf of Mexico, and Malaysia). DO significant exposure to the new Brazilian off shore oil field with 8 rigs contracted in the region, and new activity isn't expected to meaningfully peak until 2015. The company also has limited exposure to the declining fields in the North Sea, with only 3 contracted rigs (1 of which was contracted by a firm that just filled for bankruptcy in Britain and will be relocated).

There is approximately 174 semisubmersible platforms and drill ships available to be contracted from off-shore drilling companies (excludes rigs owned by integrated oil companies). I estimate that DO controls 17% of the market, with Transocean as the largest competitor. It is estimated that there are approximately 20 new deep sea rigs that have been commissioned to be built, including 10 from Transocean. This is an attractive market because it is (1) limited to a handful of players and long-term contracts that gives these firms bargaining power over their customers, and (2) the large capital required to add new rigs to the market represents a significant barrier to entry.

Company	Rigs	Share
Diamond	**31**	**17.8%**
Transocean	78	44.8%
Pride	17	9.8%
Noble	16	9.2%
Sea Drill	14	8.0%
Other	18	10.3%
Total	174	100.0%

In my opinion DO is the best positioned offshore drilling company in the industry. They benefit from having the best mix of semisubmersibles as a percentage of their total fleet (70%, which also represents 85% of DO revenues). This advantage gives DO the highest average day rates in the industry. They are also in the best financial condition with the lowest debt as a percentage of enterprise value (there primary competitor, Transocean has a significant debt burden that could constrain their operation given the credit freeze). They generate the highest return on capital and the highest free cash flow per dollar of revenue. Their strategy of upgrading mid-sea semisubmersible rigs (<4,000 ft) to deep sea rigs (+7,500 ft) is significantly less costly than building new deep-sea rigs from scratch, and the strategy is paying off. Below is a comparison of the major industry players.

	Revenue	Gross Margin	Profit Margin	Free Cash Flow	Return on Capital Employed	Debt as % of EV	Floating Rigs	% of Fleet Floating	Forward P/E	Dividend Yield
Diamond	$3,544	64.7%	37.0%	$953	17.5%	5.8%	31	68.9%	6.73	10.2%
Transocean	$12,674	57.8%	33.2%	$2,751	7.0%	44.6%	44	30.1%	4.88	0.0%
Noble	$3,447	67.1%	45.3%	$698	12.5%	13.7%	13	20.6%	4.55	0.7%
ENSCO	$2,450	67.3%	47.0%	$385	12.0%	8.9%	5	10.0%	5.48	0.4%
Rowan	$2,213	43.3%	19.3%	($135)	7.5%	26.2%	0	0.0%	6.51	0.0%
Atwood	$527	58.8%	40.7%	($136)	10.5%	23.6%	6	54.5%	4.35	0.0%
Pride	$2,310	51.2%	36.9%	($140)	16.6%	23.0%	17	38.6%	7.53	0.0%

Economics & Strategy:

DO's primary strategy has been to upgrade mid-water semisubmersible rigs to ultra deep rigs. The spread on the day rate between mid-water and deep-sea platforms is approximately $100K per day. Refurbishing existing rigs is significantly cheaper than building new rigs from scratch. Refurbishing a rig cost approximately $300 million. The deep sea rigs command day rates in excess of 500K per day and the market for these rigs is less competitive due to the high cost of building deep-sea rigs. The existing market capacity should remain tight for the foreseeable future as there is much stronger demand from oil companies for deep-sea capabilities. In short, I don't expect the day rates for these rigs to decrease significantly in the near term, 1- 3 years. Moreover, many of DO's contracts are long term and they should be able to maintain Revenues in excess of $3 billion for the next 3-5 years if oil stays at $50 or greater.

Controversy:

A.   If oil prices stabilize at less than $50 barrel for next several years, day rates will decrease causing DO's revenues and profits will begin falling around 2011. This is the primary concern of investors that drove the stock down 50% following the low crude prices over the course of this winter.

B.   DO has 9 jack-up rigs in the Golf of Mexico (GOM). 1 GOM rig is currently un-leased and 5 have leases that terminate in mid 2009. Day rates for these Rigs is approximately $130K and cost $45K. However this business represents around 10% of their revenues.

Reason to Own:

A.   DO operates a great business in an attractive industry that will generate strong sustainable cash flows for the foreseeable future. The company is generating a 10 year ROIC of 17.5% which is around double my estimate of their cost of capital. The company has generated an average free cash flow of $575 million over the last 3 years (annual ROIC of 25%) even accounting for heavy capital expenditures of $550-$650 million each year. Future CAPEX will decrease over the next 3 years as DO only has 2 more semisubmersibles that could to be upgraded to work in deeper oceans. With all of 2009 and 70% of 2010 already under contract, oil above $50, and an estimated maintenance CAPEX of $150; it is quite reasonable that DO can produced a annual free cash flow of approximately $800 to $1100 in the future.

B.   DO has a company policy that it pays out all of its excess free cash flow as special dividends. My projection of future cash flows can support a 10% dividend yield going forward. Buying the stock today, you could possibly recoup your entire investment in the company through cash dividends over the next 10 years, and in effect own the company for free (my kind of investment!) DO has a normal dividend of $0.50 per share (0.8% yield) and has paid special dividends of; $5.75 in 2007, $6.23 in 2008, and is on track to pay out $7.50 in 2009.

C.   DO has a shareholder friendly management and board. DO operates as a subsidiary of the Loews Company (50.4%

ownership) which is owned by the Tische company, and has a long history of being focused on maximizing shareholder value. The company has never done any acquisitions, and as mentioned earlier returns all excess cash to shareholders. DO doesn't have any issue related to excessive executive pay, options, or questionable related party transactions.

D.   Investing in DO (an off-shore oil driller) will provide a good hedge against Federal Reserve Monetary Policy reigniting inflation, as this will lower value of dollar and thus increase value of crude oil and ensure high day rates. Also a good hedge against higher energy prices as a result of potential supply-demand mismatches as global economic activity recovers.

Valuation:

DO currently trades for $68.96 per share ($9.6 billion market cap) representing a trailing and forward P/E of $7.3x and 6.8x respectively. Below I have valued the company using 3 different approaches (1) normalized earnings and P/E, (2) simple discounted cash flow model, and (3) replacement cost. All three valuation techniques reach similar valuation ranges. I believe the value of DO is between of $75-$95 per share.

Normalized Earnings and P/E

Determining a normalized earnings estimate for DO is difficult for two reasons, (1) volatility in crude prices and thus day rates and (2) the effect on fleet wide average day rates through the conversion of mid water rigs to deep water.

Value Investing: A Disciplined Framework

First off, it is impossible to accurately forecast oil rigs, but futures contracts and energy industry commentators believe oil may stabilize around $50 per barrel. If oil prices stabilize around 50 dollars deep sea day rates may stabilize around $400K per day, and mid-sea day rates around $300K. At the same time the new emphasis by integrated oil companies on deep-water exploration should continue to drive higher levels of rig utilization. Over the last three years DO has also upgraded 6 mid sea semisubmersibles to deep-sea highly specialized rigs, including 3 in late 2007 and 2008 that can drill at 10,000 feet commanding the highest dayrates ($650K) and longest contracts. The upgraded fleet will contribute to a much higher fleet-wide day rate than the company experienced pre-2006.

Accounting for oil prices around $50, the updated family of rigs, and current contract information, I estimate that normalized revenues for DO would be approximately $3 billion (a 15% discount to 2008 revenue). Assuming a normalized net income margin of 29%-32% (most cost are fixed), DO would generate normalized earnings in the range of $6.25-6.90 per share once existing contracts with higher day rates run their course over the next 3 years. Given the attractiveness of DO's business model, high profit margins, and ability to generate substantial cash; I believe a normalized P/E of 12-14 would be appropriate. This would result in a valuation range of $75-$95 per share. Please note that the current market expectations for 2009 and 2010 are $10.38 and $10.16 respectively (given today's stock price, the market had been discounting post 2010 earnings given oil's trading rang of $30-$50 this winter).

Simple Discounted Cash Flow Model

A better approach may be to calculate a valuation using a discounted cash flow model. Below is a simple free cash flow model that assumes the price of oil remains in the $30-$50 dollar a barrel range through the end of 2011, and than remains above $50 beginning in 2012 and beyond. As a caveat, I can't predict oil prices, but in my opinion this scenario seems reasonable give the projects for future oil demand, and are most likely too conservative vs. overly optimistic. The model below results in an $88 per share valuation using a 10% required rate of return (discount rate). This represents a $28% appreciation from today's market price. Please note that the 2011-2015 CAPEX represents a conservative level of expenditures twice my estimate of maintenance CAPEX requirements, as I am assuming the last of the 2 potential rig upgrades is completed in 2010.

	2009	2010	2011	2012	2013	2014	2015	TV
Cash from Ops.	$1,500	$1,300	$800	$1,000	$1,100	$1,400	$1,500	
Capital Expenditure	($470)	($300)	($300)	($300)	($300)	($300)	($300)	
Free Cash Flow	$1,030	$1,000	$500	$700	$800	$1,100	$1,200	$12,000
Discounted at 10%	$982	$867	$394	$501	$521	$651	$646	$6,158
NPV	$10,720							
Net Cash	237							
Total Value	$10,957							
Shares Outstanding	139							
Value per share	**$78.83**							

Replacement cost

Another way to consider the value of the company would be to calculate the replacement cost of DO's rigs. The conservative costs to build new rigs are: deep-sea rig cost $400 million, mid-sea rig cost $300, drill ship $500 million, and jack-up rigs $125. Thus the conservative replacement value of DO's rigs would be approximately $12,350 or $88 dollars per share. To provide a margin of error I have not included DO's 8 story 182,000 square foot Houston office building, Louisiana property and facilities, or $237 million net cash position.

Financial Strength:

DO is very strong financially with net cash position of $237 million, and debt/total capitalization of 5.8%. The company's financial health should remain strong as evidence of their $10.3 billion backlog that is approximately 3 years of revenue at 2008 levels. DO has the ability to generate annual free cash flows of $600-$1,100, which is more than adequate to cover CAPEX and dividends. I estimate DO's maintenance CAPEX to be approximately $150 million, and since 1997 DO has never generated operating cash flow below this mark. DO has $503 million of debt outstanding of which half matures in 2014, with the remainder in 2015. DO generates enough free cash flow to pay off this debt in less than a year.

Carpenter Technology Corp (CRS)

Executive Summary:

Carpenter Technology Corporation (CRS) currently trades at $16.71 per share. The company is a cyclical business and the market is rewarding a 10x forward P/E ratio on depressed earnings. I believe the company is extremely undervalued. I estimate the intrinsic value to be in a range of 38-$54 per share representing a 55% margin of safety. Wall Street's concerns with CRS are very short term in nature and the long run outlook for CRS is strong. The company is financially sound and they have developed a strong sustainable competitive position by successfully carving out a niche in the specialty alloy segment. Moreover, the company is extremely financially sound and is not at risk of going out of business. Additionally, the stock pays a 4.3% dividend yield, and produces ample operating cash flow to cover future dividend payments and CAPEX.

Corporate Overview:

CRS is a leading international manufacturer and distributor of specialty alloys, powder alloys, and titanium serving the aerospace (37%), industrial (23%), automotive (12%), consumer products (11%), energy (10%), and medical (7%) industries. Fiscal year 2008 revenues were $1.95 billion and income from continuing operations was $200 million (10% of sales). No customer makes up more than 10% of sales. International sales comprise 34% of revenue and have been increasing at a 27% CAGR since 2003. 56% of international sales are to Europe, and 18% are to Canada and Mexico. Approximately 110 of CRS's 3,400 employees are unionized and they are localized to one manufacturing plant and their agreement expires in 2013. Over the past 3 years CRS has sold around 110,000 tons of metal products each year, and generated over $200 million in free cash flow

	1999	2000	2001	2002	2003	2004	2005	2006	2007	2008	10 Year Average
Total Revenue	$1,049	$1,109	$1,324	$977	$871	$1,017	$1,314	$1,465	$1,839	$1,954	$1,292
Gross Margin	23.0%	22.3%	21.6%	16.7%	17.6%	18.2%	24.1%	27.3%	23.2%	23.4%	21.8%
Adj. Net Income Margin	3.5%	4.8%	2.9%	(3.6%)	(1.3%)	3.5%	10.3%	14.5%	12.4%	14.2%	6.1%
Cash from Ops.	$87	$62	$119	$144	$92	$94	$143	$238	$275	$219	$147
Capital Expenditure	($153)	($105)	($51)	($27)	($9)	($8)	($14)	($9)	($47)	($119)	($55)
Free Cash Flow	($66)	($43)	$68	$117	$84	$86	$129	$218	$228	$100	$92
Free Cash Flow Margin	(6.3%)	(3.8%)	5.%	12.0%	9.6%	8.5%	9.8%	14.9%	12.4%	5.1%	7.1%
Return on Assets	3.7%	3.7%	4.8%	0.8%	1.4%	3.0%	7.9%	10.4%	9.9%	9.8%	5.5%
Return on Capital	5.3%	5.3%	6.9%	1.2%	2.3%	4.8%	12.5%	15.7%	14.5%	14.5%	8.3%
Return on Equity	5.7%	8.3%	5.4%	(1.0%)	(2.2%)	7.1%	21.5%	24.0%	21.4%	21.0%	11.1%

Industry & Competitive Position:

The steel industry is highly competitive and fragmented. CRS is focused on specialty alloys and stainless steel. The company has successful carved out a niche market for highly

95

engineered materials for customized demanding applications. CRS has focused on niche markets that require high levels of sophistication and customization. The company's experience and reputation for manufacturing expertise has created strong customer relationships and high barriers to entry.

CRS believes there are ten primary domestic competitors who make one or more of the products that CRS produces. These competitors are primarily competing in the stainless steel product category (34% of CRS revenues). Public competitors include Allegheny Technology (ATI), Haynes International (HAYN), and Precision Castparts (PCP).

Economics & Strategy:

CRS's growth strategy has been focused on expanding to new emerging markets in Asia. Separately, the company uses their service and design centers near their customer locations and promote strong relationships with their customers by co-designing complex components (which eliminates bidding), and offering just in time delivery (which has fused CRS into the supply chain of their customers, making it difficult and expensive to change suppliers).

CRS has been successful passing through raw material prices by using price surcharges, indexing mechanisms, and base price adjustments to manage their exposure to volatile commodity prices. CRS owns their manufacturing facilities but leases their corporate headquarters and service/distribution centers. Their business isn't capital intensive one plants are in place. I estimate that maintenance CAPEX is $20 million.

Reason to Own:

A.   The company has generated strong returns on capital including an ROA of 15.6%, ROE of 29.1%, and a ROIC of 22.9%.

B.   CRS has been returning excess cash to shareholders. The company has a 4.3% dividend yield. In the last 2 years CRS has repurchased $450 million in shares and still has $50 million remaining on existing share repurchase programs.

C.   Insiders have decidedly turned bullish and have begun repurchasing shares in the $25-$40 dollar range in September and August. In 2007 most insiders were selling shares when they were north of $60 per share.

Concerns:

A.   CRS's business has historically been very cyclical. The company lost money in 2002 and 2003. If the global economic situation worsens and demand for the CRS's end product market falls, near term earnings could decrease. However, CRS did divest most of their businesses that performed poorly in the last recession. Today only 35% of their revenues are related to commoditized product (stainless steel) versus highly specialized alloys.

B.   Company repurchased shares at high prices even though management was selling stock. The company most recently repurchased $450 million of shares at an average of $56 a share (almost double today's price).

C.   50% of CRS revenues are in the aerospace and automotive sectors. The companies in the industries are having near term difficulties including the strike at Boeing, delays in new plane programs at Boeing and Airbus, and the fall in vehicle sales. However, in the long term these industries will continue to expand globally, and CRS is positioned well to benefit.

D.   A one-time increase in pension expense of $0.28 per share, and a booked reserve for environmental litigation of $0.08 per share additionally spooked investors.

E.   35% of CRS revenues are related to stainless steel. Stainless steel is a substitute for nickel, and as nickel price rose through the first half of 2008 demand for stainless steel fell. Since then nickel prices have retreated. If prices stay low, demand for stainless steel will fall, impacting revenue and profits.

F.   CRS had been receiving $8-4 million ($0.18-$0.09 per share) per year in government subsidies from anti dumping tariffs on stainless steel. These subsidies will no longer be paid to CRS going forward.

Valuation:

CRS is currently trading for $16.71 per share at a new 52 week low (52 week range: $61.78-$11.72) at a trailing P/E of 3.5x and a forward P/E of 10.8x. I believe normalized earnings are between $3.50 and $4.00 per share (before additional share repurchases), consensus is $1.57 per share in fiscal 2009 and around $1.55 in fiscal 2010. Due to the cyclical nature of CRS's business and near term flat growth prospects, a 9-12x P/E multiple would be appropriate. Based on my estimation of normalized earnings and adding back $6.80 per share in net cash, the intrinsic value of the stock would be in a range of $38-$54 per share.

Normalized Revenue ($MM)	$1,563	$1,563
Adj. Normal Income Margin	10.0%	10.0%
Normalized Earnings	$156	$156
Shares Outstanding (MM)	44.06	44.06
Normalized EPS	$3.55	$3.55
P/E Multiple	9.0	12.0
Value of Shares	$31.92	$42.56
Net Cash per Share	$6.74	$6.74
Total Value per Share	**$38.66**	**$49.30**

Financial Strength:

I believe CRS is financially strong. CRS has a net debt of ($300) million comprised of $600 million in cash and short term investments and $300 million in debt, of which $23 million is due in 2009, $20 million in 2010, $100 million in 2012, $100 million in 2013, and the remaining $57 million in 2018. Additionally, the company has $138 million unused credit revolver that expires in August 2010. The company has a BBB credit rating. CRS has been paying down debt since 2000 when net debt was $573 million. The company has adequate resources to fund operations and CAPEX, and continue to pay their dividend and pay down debt. The company has a quick ratio of 1.73x. The company also has a small pension fund which is well funded.

Value Investing: A Disciplined Framework

About the Author

Tyler Hardt, CFA is the Founder, Portfolio Manager, and Managing Member of Pelican Bay Capital Management, LLC. Mr. Hardt has 10 year of investment management experience and is the lead Portfolio Manager for all 3 of Pelican Bay Capital Management's portfolios. Prior to founding Pelican Bay Capital Management, Mr. Hardt spent 9 years as an Equity Analyst on the Domestic Value Team at Artisan Partners Asset Management. Mr. Hardt has also held Corporate Mergers & Acquisitions and Corporate Strategy roles at AT&T and American Tire Distributors. Mr. Hardt received his MBA with Honors from the Wharton School at the University of Pennsylvania. He graduated Cum Laude from the University of Maryland with a Bachelor of Science in Finance. Mr. Hardt lives in Naples, Florida.

For more information please visit www.pelicanbaycap.com